...JUST WORK!

MORE THAN A JOB, FULFILMENT

an international primer to employment

Maurizio Fantato

Henk Vaars

Mediadunes

…Just work!

Acknowledgements:

David Colón (cover design) - A book's cover is the first thing a potential reader sees and it can make a lasting impression. http://colonfilm.com

Shelly Greenhalgh-Davis (proofreading) - More than just proofreading and from a writer in her own terms http://shellydavisbooks.com

Tina Scarpelli McGugan for her useful introductions in the USA

Cecelia Haddad for her own introductions Down Under

Our wives and families for their patience.

Skype as an invaluable tool for online collaboration.

Dedicated to Marcel Elte who passed away suddenly and unexpectedly just days before this book was due to be published. His contribution lives on.

This edition first published in 2015

Copyright © Maurizio Fantato, Henk Vaars

All rights reserved. No part of this publication may be reproduced, stored or transmitted in any format and by any means except as expressly permitted by law or without prior permission from the publisher or authors.

FOREWORD

Previously having been a board director for one of the largest of the UK's employment agencies, I recognise the challenges faced by individuals in their job seeking and their career development. Having advised friends and colleagues in the development of their CVs into a fit for purpose selling document, I can also understand the feeling of inadequacy that some can face when having to communicate their experience and their strengths in a succinct yet meaningful manner.

The issue arises because, for most people, changing jobs (or careers) is not a regular event. Any lessons learned from previous events are quickly lost when undertaking similar actions does not arise on a frequent basis. Not only is this often the case, but, usually, when an individual is considering a job or career change, he or she is doing so with a variety of emotions swirling around. These can involve issues concerning finance, self-esteem (especially if the change is not of the individual's making) and emotions (particularly if the individual has to explain the change to family members and seek their commitment to possible changes). So it would not be surprising if the individual concerned is in a state of mild panic and rushes at the range of actions that need to be taken.

When such changes have happened to me, I had to think through my course of actions for myself. The beauty of "Just Work" is that it addresses the challenges and provides possible course of action for each of them. What is more it does so with a light touch that makes it an easy read!

Whilst some readers may wish to dip in and out of the book, my suggestion is that there is benefit in reading it cover to cover. My reasoning is that the contributors cover not only the practicalities but also address developments in different job markets and different career paths. By reading the entire book the reader will be better prepared for all eventualities and is likely to learn more about the range of opportunities facing him or herself. Even if you have a clear plan of the path you want to follow, I suggest reading the book thoroughly will better prepare you to make a success of following that path.

I congratulate the authors for producing a book that should benefit all those that read it. The old adage of "fail to plan, plan to fail" is as valid in an individual's job hunting as it is in the strategic development of an international corporation. For those of you considering a change of job or of career, read on, plan well, make the right choice and be a success!

Tony Hoskins

December 2014

Tony Hoskins is a strategic thinker, international consultant, researcher with The Work Foundation, the RSA, the DTI and CIPD, accomplished speaker on CSR and the impact of narrative reporting, reputation management expert, as well as author of many articles on the subject of work, employment, corporate governance and reputation management. He has written five books.

...Just work!

PREFACE

It was a bleak mid-autumn evening in southern England; a storm was raging and rain was lashing against the windows. Trees, set in the orange glow of streetlamps and now almost bereft of their leaves, were casting dancing shadows on the tarmac. Lights suddenly flickered; there was a knock at the door, and a small parcel fell with a thud on the porch floor.

We tried to romanticise how this book was started, but the truth is that, like similar ventures, it all began with a conversation among friends. Maurizio had recently come out of a less-than-pleasant work experience and was looking for a new opportunity. Henk had also just finished managing a leading HR operation in the Netherlands.

Both had written a few blogs. Some of these articles were about giving tips to candidates on key job-hunting aspects. So one day, in the course of a longer-than-usual Skype call, they came up with the idea of pooling those existing articles, plus a few more that they already had in planning, and serving them in a longer and more structured version. They toyed with the idea of a website, but wanted to offer something more original than the usual how-to manual, something with more individuality and an international flavour, aimed at candidates willing to stretch themselves and to embrace the opportunities offered by a more globalised economy.

Several Skype calls later and after many shared documents in Google Drive, they realised that they had sufficient material for a useful eBook. A title and a cover followed suit. Contributors were sought; many applied but few were chosen. A half dozen eggs later, with the addition of some organic vanilla essence and a good blast in the digital fan oven, this book came to light.

We hope you'll have as much fun reading it as we had writing it. We hope you will find that dream job, but above all, we hope this book may help you discover something of yourself that you didn't know you had. If we achieved this objective we would be very satisfied indeed.

Finally, quite aside from our best wishes, we'd like to hear from you. We both strongly believe that the networking opportunities provided by the web through all its channels can enrich us and create uniquely dynamic loops - circles of friends and co-workers seeking to create something new or improve existing processes. So if you share our vision, do get in touch.

November 2014

AUTHORS & CONTRIBUTORS
Maurizio Fantato

In his mid-fifties and with a rich and varied experience of working in the Americas, as well as in several EU countries, many years of advanced marketing communication, a passion for writing and for community outreach, Maurizio brings to this book not merely a vision for finding work at the international level, but real first-hand experience.

He is currently a freelance consultant on digital media and all things new on the Internet, as well as being the trustee of two charities, an avid blogger, the founder of a civic society on sustainable transport in his district, a local candidate for the Green Party, and an active Fellow of the Royal Society of Arts, among several other things. He has a son and a wife, who put up with him and all his multifaceted interests.

http://www.mediadunes.com/maurizio-fantato.html

Henk Vaars

Is there such thing as a professional job hopper? Job hopping could be the single biggest obstacle for job seekers. Yet when you become a pro, like Henk, you can continue to find jobs. After years in a variety of posts, Henk landed himself a job as a location manager for a temporary staffing agency. Being in the middle of the recruitment world - on the other side of the fence - he became fascinated by a new recruitment phenomenon called pre-recorded web-based video-interviewing. This is a plugin for applicant tracking software systems, and he ended up managing one for the recruitment software companies specialising in that service. In the software industry there is one truth: Once you're in - you're in! So right now, though in a different market, Henk is still dealing with software, but as a commercial advisor for a well-known IT company in the Netherlands.

http://www.mediadunes.com/henk-vaars.html

Contributors:

(Australia) Peter Ambrose is Associate Director of Ardus Consulting, a search and recruitment consultancy established in Australia since 1995. Peter has 13 years' experience in recruitment in Australia. Peter's career transitioned through engineering to senior industrial sales and marketing roles with BHP, Brambles and CSR Building Products. Since 2001 has engaged in executive search and recruitment with Ardus Consulting across a number of sectors - building products, engineering, resources, environmental, retail and manufacturing. Mid to senior level appointments including sales, marketing, financial services, operations, manufacturing, logistics and engineering. Degree qualified in Civil Engineering supported by postgraduate university qualification in Marketing. Peter enjoys living in Sydney with its cosmopolitan lifestyle, beaches and sporting events.

https://au.linkedin.com/pub/peter-ambrose/3/aa5/932

(Netherlands) Marcel Elte's long career consists of

combined management and business diplomacy skills both internationally and in Holland, his country of birth and day to day operational base. From specialising in bridging computer information technology with the development of applied digital medical diagnostics Marcel moved into advanced management, feeling that his strengths were more people focussed, at all levels of employment, education or background. This became his main occupation for the last 25 years. His specialism is bringing the best out of people, stimulating individual qualities that support a shift to the desired changes, maintaining a close link with a person's interests. His focus being always on individual values in support of a professional goal. His motto is, 'One who does not change his ideas does not think'.

http://www.winwinwerkt.nl

(Netherlands) Arnold Fontijn is a personal coach, image consultant and interior designer. This unique blend of skills make him focus on how an individual can radiate their true personality, highlighting the positive skills that may otherwise be hidden behind the 'wrong' outer image. His goal is to present people at their best, comfortable with themselves so that they can be more confident and therefore more creative too. He has been managing his own coaching and design company Image- & InterieurProof for some years now, offering bespoke image consultancy advice.

https://www.linkedin.com/in/arnoldfontijn -
http://www.image-en-interieurproof.nl

(USA) Evan Parris is a Recruiter and Employment Specialist with over ten years of experience in recruitment and retention, business development, sales and marketing, vocational rehabilitation and establishing partnerships among local businesses and non-profit groups. He is the co-founder of the Greater Kansas City Employment Nexus, a consortium of employers, service providers, vocational counsellors and community advocates that meet monthly to discuss employment trends, share job leads, and develop opportunities for companies to target unemployed veterans and job-seekers with disabilities who are traditionally faced with employment challenges. The Nexus received the 2013 Award for Outstanding Community Service from the Missouri Rehabilitation Association and was awarded a nationally recognized grant for organizations dedicated to improving job opportunities for individuals with disabilities.

https://www.linkedin.com/in/evanparris

(Netherlands) Jorien Stoop is a strategic, multidisciplinary project leader with an eye for innovation and perfection. Her skill set is vast, but her greatest expertise is in understanding clients' needs, translating them into deliverables for the Dutch logistic service provider she is working for. In April 2014 Jorien set up a coaching programme with Henk Vaars, co-author of ...Just Work! https://www.linkedin.com/in/jorienstoop

...Just work!

INTRODUCTION

It seems fitting to write an introduction even if this is supposed to be a different kind of book, moving away from the usual stereotypes yet on a very popular and truly life-changing subject. You are, after all, unlikely to be interested in this book if you aren't considering finding a new job, aren't worried about your present career, aren't actively seeking employment, or have been unsuccessful in your quest and wish to review your present situation in order to understand where you may have gone wrong.

One of the paradoxes of today's world is that we are surrounded by heaps of information yet are often less capable of making the right decision. Much of the stuff we are going to tell you could be found strewn across countless online channels (what couldn't?), yet we have less time to digest it all. How do we sift through such quagmire of data and information, really focussing on what matters to our present circumstances? The more we look, the more daunting the task ahead might seem. We all want to get a grip on a solution speedily, which is what we have been attempting to do in this book, offering a quick digest of essential tools to get started again, a bit like pressing ctrl+alt+del on your old PC...

In trying to explain what this book is in the shortest possible way, we thought we'd tell you also what we didn't want to write about. We didn't want to compile a personal eulogy offering advice focussed on our own experiences only. Such knowledge would get you nowhere, which is why we teamed up with other professionals, and not just those who have contributed directly but many more. Many of the experts and contributors were from different parts of the world and from a variety of disciplines. This is one the traits that makes this book different and of more universal appeal.

However, much as we would have liked it, in the short space available through the next pages we simply couldn't pretend to offer you a full life guidance manual. Nevertheless, we made every attempt to steer you in a direction that wouldn't just get you to any job, but hopefully take you to a new and more rewarding life adventure. Our greatest satisfaction would be to know that we may have led you to your own eureka moment, whether that meant starting anew, just getting your dream job, or even considering getting further professional help.

Though the quest for serendipity is also beyond the scope of this book, we aimed to fine tune your senses. We cannot magically change your circumstances, but sometimes if we are afflicted by problems we may become blind to opportunities ahead of us. We may be in the desert, thirsty and slowly dehydrating yet failing to see the nomad's caravan on the horizon just because we are too closely focussing on ourselves.

So what is this book about in a nutshell? We have three simple objectives. The first is to get you to pause for a moment before you embark on finding a new job, asking yourself some questions about what you really want to achieve and whether that road will be one to happiness. The second is to provide you with a succinct and highly

...Just work!

practical way of going through all the tools available out there, giving you the best advice on how to maximise effectiveness. Finally, we wanted this primer to have an international dimension and not simply to reflect our interests and backgrounds, but to mirror today's circumstances. We live in a world that is shrinking rapidly thanks to advanced communications methods. That perfect job is rarely, if ever, on your doorstep. Comparing your experience with circumstances elsewhere might help you put things into perspective. This, and hopefully more, is what this book is about.

If while reading *Just Work!* you begin to find something of your true self, rekindling the same inner fire that inspired those valiant knights of old, we are certain that you will have no qualms in facing and defeating any dragon that may come your way. And at long last, that personal Holy Grail, whatever it might possibly be, could truly be within your reach. The tools provided in this book are your personal weapons. They will help you, but only if you discover, nurture, and believe in your true self.

We wish you the best of luck in your quest and a life choice that will truly reflect what a wonderful and deserving human being you really are.

Henk, Maurizio, and all the contributors

December 2014

CONTENTS

Foreword 4
Preface 6
Authors & contributors 8
Introduction 12
Basic preparation 21
   A quick-start guide 23
   Must have - online skills and tools 25
   Get organised - do it right 27
      Don't overdo it! 29
   Your personal network 31
      Friends and family 31
   Your career path 33
      Get rid of negative emotions 33
      Looking back 34
      Deriving enjoyment 35
Working for yourself or someone else? 37
      Going solo - be prepared 37
      Which way? 39
Finding a job when you are over 50 40
   The big question 44
Starting a new life - abroad 45
   You are going to carry a lot of baggage… 45

- Preparation is key 49
- Job seeking in Australia 51
  - Setting the stage 51
  - More recent times......the pervasive Internet 51
  - "Headhunting" 55
  - Applying for a job 55
  - Recruitment tool - testing 56
  - Medical check 56
  - Reference checking 56
  - Australian Trends 57
- A US perspective on job hunting in the twenty-first century 59
  - From seeker to hunter gatherer 59
  - Network, network, network 62
  - USA favorite tools 64
  - Go after medium/small fish 65
  - Thinking of moving to the U.S.? 68
  - There is social, and 'social' 69
- How the HR industry really works… 73
  - Employer branding vs. personal branding 73
  - Blazing hot tips on keywords 75
  - Tracking your profile via social media 75
  - Recruitment events and HR conferences 76

- HR industry blogs 77
- Smarten up your act with search aggregators 77
- The paradox of choice 78
- The selection process 79
  - How do recruiters select? 79
- Temporary work and agencies 81
- Career coaches 85
  - Why hire a career coach? 85
- Tools of the trade 87
  - Your own web presence 87
  - Leveraging the power of social media 89
    - Back to basic 90
    - All about image 91
  - Clean up your act first 91
    - Facebook 91
    - Google+ 92
    - YouTube 92
    - LinkedIn 92
    - Twitter 93
    - Sparkling new media presence 93
  - Channel-by-channel action 94
    - Facebook - to gain intelligence only 94
    - Twitter - if you must 95

...Just work!

    LinkedIn - your job search companion 95

    Google+ 96

    Skype 96

    Google Hangouts 97

Job boards 98

    Seconds rather than minutes 98

    The 'right' job only 99

Your CV 101

    What your CV should be for 101

    What kind of CV? 101

    How many pages? 102

    Designer or boring? 103

    Should I go digital? 104

    Critical CV elements 104

    Should I insert references? 105

    Should I have a photograph? 105

    How many versions? 105

    ...finally 106

The cover note 108

    Key ingredients 109

Selling product "you" 111

    Your personal value proposition 113

    Developing a winning value proposition 114

Distance yourself from criticism 120

Getting to talk to someone 120

Creating effective lists 122

Telephone manners 123

Extrovert or introvert? 124

Personal reflections on getting that 'perfect' job 126

    Turning point 127

    Networking 127

    Breaking the ice 128

    Sealing the deal 128

The interview process 130

    The first interview 130

        Live video interviews 132

        Pre-recorded video interviews 133

    What would you do with a million Ping-Pong balls? .. 134

    What to say if a recruiter calls 135

    Expect question like… 135

    Clothes do make the man, or woman! 142

        Who can make the difference? 142

        Presenting who you really are 143

        Exuding confidence 143

        First impressions 145

        Total look 146

    A suit for every occasion 146

    What suits you best 152

    You are you own calling card! 154

  The assessment centre 155

  The second interview 159

  The thank-you note 160

The job offer 162

In the end it's all down to your imagination… 164

  A word about 'positive' thinking 166

  ...One final hint - the new economy 169

BASIC PREPARATION

So what do you need to do before you rush about making calls, registering for all job sites on the planet, and writing about 100 versions of your CV?

Well, the obvious question you need to ask yourself is, what sort of job are you looking for? We know you need to work - bills need paying, your home may be mortgaged, and so on. But do you want to go back to your previous occupation, or is this perhaps a time to reassess your career and consider different pathways? You may wish to think about self-employment, for example. Or, if you have spent the last thirty years or so working, you may even consider semi-retirement. Everyone's circumstances are different. We can't tell you what is right or wrong for you. But please do take at least a few days to consider your own circumstances. Write down what you need and then write down on a separate piece of paper what you would like to have. Then take another paper and write down the kind of jobs you may consider and whether these fulfill the 'needs' requirement, or the 'would like' section. Rate these jobs and then leave all this behind. Take yourself off for a couple of days, especially if you have just lost your job, do something you truly love, and get back to those papers on your return. Look at your findings, comparing with your present outlook. Do they still match or are you now thinking of taking yourself into a different direction?

...Just work!

Take a little time on the above exercise. If you are uncertain, again, do something else and get back to this exercise. As long as you don't spend your life doing this, it's a worthwhile thing to do. Success in job finding is mainly based on beliefs about yourself. Believe in yourself and in what you really want to achieve and you stand a greater chance of succeeding. If you don't know what you want, you're much less likely to get something that will satisfy you. A job gained in unclear circumstances, just because you need something, may lead you nowhere or may take you back to the beginning of this chapter, and what you must avoid at all cost is a continuous cycle of employment and unemployment. We all strive for harmony and balance, and a state of continuous imbalance brought about by sudden changes and too many ups and downs is bound to hurt us deeply, then our way out of troubles may become even more complicated and we may have to rely on additional help to get us out of trouble.

A quick-start guide

A few things you need to do before you even think about your CV.

We assume that if you are reading this book, it is because you are either stuck in your current job and you need to find a way out of it, or you lost your employment through redundancy or dismissal. If you have moved seamlessly from one position to another, you clearly do not need to read this book, unless you have a passion for books on employment, of course, and who are we to judge?

Once you have decided that you need to look for work and even before you start applying, you have to do a little housekeeping: Google yourself. Okay, you may not like Google (really?) then use Bing or Yahoo. It doesn't matter, but check out whatever comes up when someone is looking for you. Now that you have done this what can you see? Are you satisfied with the accuracy of the information? Can you see some stuff that perhaps you foolishly put into one of your social media accounts when you were eighteen and you now regret it? Don't omit looking at images! You never know. Some of your friends may have tagged you in a less-than-flattering pose, or worse.

To be on the safe side you should even ask a friend to do the same for you and to report back. If, like us, your online life is very complicated, you may need to enter this information into a matrix, using a spreadsheet or a piece of paper. Don't get hung up about the method. It's all about the delivery.

...Just work!

You now have a good overall view of how a prospective employer will find you. If you're satisfied with what you see, give yourself a good pat on the back and move on to the next chapter. If not, this is the time to put things right, and I am afraid this aspect of the operation may take you anything from a couple of hours to a few days, depending on the damage limitation/revamp exercise you need to carry out, but omit this at your peril. It won't matter how good your CV, cover letter, video presentation, etc. is if what they find out online is bad. You're simply wasting your time, so put it right, now!

There are two key elements you need to focus on when you're doing online housekeeping: editorial content and visual (basically text and photographs, unless you took videos of yourself, whoops...). Take your time creating good professional content for all your social media channels and blog sites, upload professional photographs, remove inappropriate ones, and allow a few days for the search engines to spider this information, then check again.

Later on in the book we will focus in great detail on how to set up effective social media channels in case you aren't familiar with them, so don't worry too much at this stage if you don't have them or if you can't find very much about you - the essential ingredient of this chapter is that you won't find anything damaging!

By the way there are many online reputation tools out there, but you may find it useful to start from something like brandyourself.com

Must have - online skills and tools

This book started its life as an online tool, so we assumed readers' familiarity with basic computer skills. You are now holding the printed copy, but the assumption remains the same. If you really can't cope with computers you may find it hard to grasp some of the explanations and suggestions that follow in the next few chapters, but let's consider normal circumstances.

These are the basic tools for the quest you are about to undertake:

a) a computer of some kind - it doesn't matter whether it is a PC or a laptop, but you will need to write long and detailed email messages so make sure you have a keyboard and a mouse preferably. You will need to concentrate on what you are writing rather than on the tools.

b) a good Internet connection - if you don't have Internet you may miss out on jobs that are advertised and have a short shelf life, so get yourself online. If you really can't afford to be online, make sure you know of places with Wi-Fi access, like cafes, libraries, etc. near you.

c) decent word processing software - you don't need Office. You can rely on simpler tools like Google Drive or Open Office and many others, but you will need something that will allow you to present information professionally.

...Just work!

d) an email address - sounds obvious but you will need to pay attention to the email address itself. Perhaps you have a jokey email address, which is absolutely fine for your friends, like 'smellyfeet112@iname.com' or some other such delight. Well, we are sorry but an address like the one in the example will lead you nowhere in your quest for a new job. You can get as many free email accounts as you like these days, so there is no excuse for an unprofessional email address - get one now, something that boringly perhaps but effectively simply shows your name and surname. You don't need anything else.

e) optional tools - okay, so you want to be the ninja of job seekers, then you will need a few extra tools such as a camera, microphone, video editing software, a smart phone, and so on-- the list is almost endless. But it doesn't matter how good the tools are if your delivery or your content isn't up to scratch, yet if it makes you feel better, or if these tools are relevant to the posts you're applying for, by all means go ahead.

You're now almost ready to go.

Get organised - do it right

When people are looking for a job they take essentially two kinds of approaches:

a) the overdrive

b) the lazy one

Neither is effective, and the truth is, as always, in the middle.

Let us deal first with the overdrive approach. If you are the overdrive type, you will launch into the job-searching operation with gusto. You will probably sail through the first few chapters of this book, digesting its content and rushing to implement it. You will register for every job board on the face of the planet (beware of zombie sites, more later), reply to hundreds of jobs, write countless CVs, and so on. Be careful, though, as you may run the risk of burning yourself out. Furthermore, in many instances and despite what your state job centres may tell you (they just want you out of claiming benefits, they couldn't care less about your career), quality is way better than quantity. It's far better, for example, to apply well for two jobs than badly for ten. But there is another pitfall. You may end up spending all day in front of the computer and then omit other networking opportunities, such as conferences, exhibitions, or simply meeting up with other people who are still at work and may give you some inside information on posts that haven't yet been advertised. You get our drift. Besides, if you are finding yourself out of work, you really want to get out and meet people too. Do not, under any

...Just work!

circumstances, get stuck at home but take it as part of your routine that your social skills have to be kept up to scratch.

What can we say about the lazy?... Well, if your idea of looking for a job is rest and relaxation until the middle of the morning, followed by a leisurely breakfast/brunch and a long toilette in preparation for an evening out with mates, then your chances of finding a good job may be somewhat slimmer. In fact, you may not really need a job at all, and therefore you may not need to read this book either.

If you find you are somewhere in between, then this chapter could help you.

The rule of thumb is, don't spend too much of your time just looking for a job. Do other things, especially physically ones. For example, start the day with a good long jog if you can. Remember all those good intentions, like exercising, joining a gym, doing yoga, or similar? They always got put on the back burner as work and family came first. Well, you now have plenty of time on your hands and no excuses!

Once you have seen to all your physical needs, you catch up with the urgent correspondence (don't forget a good breakfast - you deserve it if you feel you have earned it!), then go out again. Yes, go out again. It doesn't matter exactly where, but leave your home and remove yourself from your computer, meeting people for a coffee perhaps, or visiting an art gallery if this is what you like, or a quick spot of shopping. Try not to spend more than an hour, then come back. Now it's time to do preparatory work to refine your work chances and apply for whatever may have come in your inbox while you were out. Do a few bits of job search at a time. In between, seek inspiration doing something constructive (no, watching TV doesn't fall into this category!), like writing a blog on your favourite subject, arranging your stamp collection, and so on. When it comes to the normal end of a working day, stop looking for work, unless of course, someone calls you urgently, and just go back to doing whatever it was you were normally doing if you had been working, like cooking, watching TV, whatever!

It's all about planning. If you plan your day effectively you will feel much better. You will feel that you deserve a chance and that you have done all you can. You can apply some vague criteria too, for example, combining the job search activities in a spreadsheet (number of applications seen, CVs sent, related activities). How you do it is for you to determine. Some people are naturally organised; others may need tools to help them on the way. The important thing is that you don't overdo it, or under-do it. Just do it right.

Don't overdo it!
If you fall in the overdrive category, you may be tempted to apply for jobs daily, regardless of whether you felt up to it (for example, you may be unwell or uninspired). Our advice is simple: don't. You will soon feel tired and overwhelmed. You may get depressed, too, as the returns on the time you have invested seldom equate to your efforts. If you feel tired, despondent, unhappy, or unwell

…Just work!

you need to break away from your job search.

While you can get away with being under the weather at work, pushing papers around or similar, you will not be able to do so when you are applying for jobs. The reason is simple. In your work environment your reputation precedes you, so your colleagues and even your boss will tolerate a little slack from time to time if you aren't feeling that wonderful because your track record is (hopefully) excellent or at least good. But nobody knows you when you are applying for a new job. So if you don't feel like writing that wonderful cover note or responding to that advert in an exemplary manner, please, don't waste your time. Make yourself a coffee, bake a cake, paint a door, take the dog for a walk, whatever. If you are unwell, take something for your cold and curl up in front of the TV. You are entitled to do so. It's much better if you recover quickly and wait until you're as bright as a button to write that job application than if you did it in a half-hearted way. If it can't be helped, don't push it.

Your personal network

Friends and family

Friends and family can often get overlooked, yet if you are fortunate enough to have some good friends or a supportive family, the onerous task of looking for employment will become much more bearable.

There are fundamentally two aspects for which you can leverage these networks, the practical side, ranging from any help like proofreading your CV or even keeping their eyes open for opportunities by using their own respective networks and the emotional one. The latter is often overlooked but it can be very important. It's almost certain that you will be working to get a job (as this can be a full-time occupation) from your home during the day. This can be a very lonely activity, and if you aren't careful you may find that you start talking to yourself or to your cat (pets, by the way, dogs in particular, can be a great help, too, in order to relieve stress at times of unemployment - cats less so as they are crepuscular creatures tending to sleep during the day). So having a few friends, particularly those who may be available during the day, could be a real bonus.

It's often better, however, to ask for specific help rather than generic help. So if you have done your introductory homework you may be able to come up with specific requests that you can then put to a selected member of your circle of friends or family.

Don't be afraid to email even those distant friends and family. They won't be upset, and even if they were, you would have gained something by knowing that you can happily remove them from your Christmas card list.

Be aware, though, of pushy friends or family members. Accept with grace an offer to take you to a job event, for example, but stop at continuous requests for updates or gratuitous career advice. In the end it doesn't really matter where you get your advice from, whether it is from a qualified counsellor or a friend, you still have to act on it, which means you need to be convinced it's the right thing to do regardless of their opinion.

At no time than while unemployed, the saying 'a friend in need is a friend indeed' is as true. You will find that the real friends and caring relatives will get closer to you, while the fair-weather friends and uninterested relations will dissipate. Take advantage of this to clean up your address book!

Finally, you may wish to look for friends through job clubs or similar networks. They can be very useful if they are already set up in your country or neighbourhood. And even if they weren't, who knows? Perhaps you may consider opening your own, provided of course, you didn't live in the middle of nowhere. But don't get yourself cut off and use the time you are looking for a job to refine your circle of friends and relatives as well as looking for new ones.

Your career path

Being unemployed is an opportunity to look back at your career. Well, it's an opportunity that has really been thrust on you, so you can't avoid it. We dislike some of the patronising language you often find in advice guides where they tell you this is a 'wonderful time for you to look back and get inspired'. Who are we kidding? Yes, of course, it may become thus, but in the beginning you are probably going through a whole raft of emotions, most negative as we assume you haven't been seeking unemployment through your own choice but through a different set of circumstances.

Get rid of negative emotions

Before you even look at your career, you need to purge yourself of negative emotions. By this we don't mean you have to seek sainthood and an ascetic life in response to any emotional damage that may have been pushed on you, but simply that you work through those emotions. Your quest for work will be greatly enriched and will have a much better chance of being successful if you harbour positive emotions in you, rather than negative ones.

So how do you do that? Well, as this isn't a counselling book we don't pretend to be able to give you an easy answer, but generally speaking, everyone has a way of dealing with these emotions. For some, hard work in the gym may be an answer; for others, a more emotional approach may be required. And if you feel like buying a voodoo doll in order to make an effigy of your former boss so that you can stick needles on it, or prefer to burn it, this

...Just work!

is entirely up to you, provided, of course, it makes you feel better.

Looking back

So you have purged yourself and can now take an objective look at your career. Start by focussing on your working life, highlighting the following:

a) the jobs you enjoyed most

b) those you hated

c) patterns (e.g. redundancy, length of employment, and so on)

Use whatever tool you may like for this simple exercise. You may write some notes, do some cards, whatever. The point is to achieve a helicopter view of your career.

When you have done all this, ask yourself a simple question: 'Do I want to pursue the same career path?' If you have answered in the affirmative, then fine. But you need to be as close to 100% confident of it. If you are hesitating, go back to the previous exercise, another day preferably, and ask yourself the same question again. If you are really stuck, you may even ask friends and family. Some of their answers may surprise you as they may tell you that when you were working for XYZ you looked really 'happy'. But please don't get too taken in by third parties - this exercise is for you only, and how people perceive you as being happy can only be subjective. Besides, they may not know that you may have had other reasons for being happy, so only you can address this issue.

If you have answered in the negative and you have found some career flaws and are unhappy with the way your working life is progressing, then this is time for you to do some more in-depth work. Before you move on, we have to tell you that these are ultimately issues only you will be able to answer. Some people are more at ease with finding an answer within themselves. For others this may be the beginning of a long journey, or for a few this is a journey that can only be done with the help of professionals. You will find out in the course of this quest to which category you belong.

Deriving enjoyment

For most people going to work is a necessary evil, unless they are self-made millionaires at the head of large corporations, in which case they are for the most part there because of their drive and passion for what they do and are therefore totally driven (e.g. Dyson). Nonetheless, regardless of what your job is, you need to find some satisfaction. It doesn't matter whether you are counting buttons or money or are writing press releases or developing websites. If you despise what you are doing, you should simply stop doing it and find something else. All well and good, you say - your circumstances may force you to be where you are (especially if you are in a penal institution, though even then you need to ask yourself why you are there). But you really need to stop it.... things will never get better if you really hate your job.

So look back at your career and pick the job you enjoyed most, or even the task within your daily routine. Can you make of it a profession? If you have answered in the affirmative, you have found a way out and you will need to focus on the following chapters.

One final word of advice. We often hear of people saying that they changed jobs because they thought it gave them an 'opening' but weren't really interested in the new post itself, just the company. For example, you go and work for an airline but you have little interest in airplanes, but just think that you may be able to be moved to another station abroad. Although these moves can happen, the truth is that if you don't do your job with total passion and commitment, sooner or later you will either be found out, or you'll simply give up. You simply cannot keep up the pretence of doing something you don't like that much for some distant reward. You are far better off in that post you may have had before, even if you got less money or weren't that glamorous, but where you were happier and felt fulfilled. Many careers have been ruined for dismissing emotions and giving too much attention to the rational mind.

WORKING FOR YOURSELF OR SOMEONE ELSE?

This is also a fundamental question you need to ask yourself at this stage. How well do you get on with people in authority? Are you happy to be led, or do you prefer to be a leader? Are you an innovator and do you have it in you to take risks? Do you have any marketable skills? Being an entrepreneur is not for the faint-hearted.

We don't pretend to give you an answer in a few lines, but if you feel inclined towards self-employment don't dismiss it. Do explore it further with the help of countless online and printed books on the subject. It doesn't really matter if in the end you decide against it. The important thing at this stage is that you take the time to assess it and agree on a direction. Going back to the drawing board is really what most of the quest for employment can be about.

Going solo - be prepared

Having explored all avenues and failed, or due to a flash of inspiration, you may decide to go solo. Be prepared for a reasonably long slog if you intend to go alone. The average time it takes for a lifestyle change is well-documented and is about five years. If you are inpatient and expect to have a breakthrough after just the first few weeks you may be disappointed.

On the other hand you may be very lucky and have an amazing breakthrough, but the statistical odds are against you, and if you are the gambling type you may not need to be reading this book and may instead need a bookmaker...

...Just work!

Going solo is a subject that is covered by almost countless publications, and there is just tons of advice out there. In some countries even governments are actively encouraging people to set up on their own, seeing the micro-economy as one of the many possible directions for improving the local economy in the context of a more complex global dimension.

Let us first say that you should never go solo (or indeed do anything else) just as an alternative to finding a job, unless you really, really want to start your business. If you start off with a negative attitude, say in response to failure, you are bound to fail, especially when you attempt to become your own boss. While there are inevitable benefits of running your own business (possibility of greater income, independency, self-fulfilment, and so on), there are also some pitfalls, such as income uncertainty at the onset and what every entrepreneur will tell you, that very soon your business will become your entire life - forget statutory holidays, or nine-to-five or taking it easy one day - being your own boss involves a great degree of self-discipline.

So here is our very basic (for the reasons we mentioned above) advice if you decided to go down this road:

a) Plan carefully, not just for the business but for your future life.

b) Involve your family and partner in the planning (you will need all their support).

c) Roll up your sleeves and be ready for the long haul and for some very hard work.

d) Seek plenty of advice (business, personal, financial).

e) Plan, plan, plan.

f) Keep a positive attitude.

Being your own boss can be hugely rewarding, but you're entering a completely different mindset, a parallel reality, and if you are successful, you will soon have to make the sort of decisions that may have led you to where you are now – life-changing decisions for other people.

Which way?

At this stage you should have reached the decision either to remain in the same career path or that the time has come for you to change. If you have decided on the latter, you would also have decided whether to go solo (get yourself a different book) or whether you want to work for someone else.

If you have decided to seek employment but using different skills, your most fundamental issue at this stage is whether you possess those skills at a sufficient level to enable you to find employment.

This may well be a simple question of highlighting them in your CV or application, but if your skills in the areas you would like to pursue are basic, you may need to retrain or gain some specific qualifications in the sectors in question. **Don't despair. This is the time to do all that.**

...Just work!

FINDING A JOB WHEN YOU ARE OVER 50

"Intentionally left blank"

Did you like that? We hope you thought it was funny. The reason why we inserted this very light-hearted joke is because if you are reading this eBook and you are over 50, your first priority is to retain a healthy sense of humour (and not just health, of course) - at all times.

Early in 2014 a renowned employment consultancy company published a survey on attitudes to finding a job between those who were about to start a career and those who were drifting towards the end of their working lives. Surprisingly, or maybe not, attitudes were strikingly similar with both cohorts perceiving to be discriminated against.

While we have a lot of sympathy for those are just starting on their career path, the task for those veering towards the sunset is inevitably much harder. Most countries have seen a large increase in unemployment of the over-fifties in the last few years, combined with the knowledge that in the coming years we have to work longer. This is a huge concern. Finding employment for the over-fifty is harder, and one of the stumbling blocks is often 'too much experience' but we shall talk about that in greater depth below.

If you are left unemployed over fifty, you can be suffering from acute shock. After all, this is the time of life when you would like to reap the benefits of your working life, and certainly not the time to make sacrifices, scrimping and saving to make ends meet. In addition, the media will play an important part in making you feel even more miserable. This is because in visual communication especially, there are very strict windows of opportunity to build a career.

...Just work!

You don't see many people over fifty in advertisements, for example, unless the services advertised are targeted specifically. Visual communicators have a very short shelf life, just like the one of Camembert cheese. However, unless you're in that specific market segment, you shouldn't worry unduly about your looks and more about your hidden skills.

So what can we suggest you do if you are over fifty and have become unemployed? Well, the original advice at the start of this book to take a good hard look at your past working life applies even more strongly to the over-fifties. Chances of re-entering the work environment in a similar role are slimmer, and this is a fact so you have essentially two options:

a) You redefine your skills and market yourself as independent consultant in your strongest areas.

b) You work fewer hours and accept that you use work to 'fill the gaps' and have more time to do things you really like. This may require, however, some readjustment in your finances.

c) You accept a lower-skill job.

e) You experiment with all three.

f) You just accept that you have reached the end of your working life and readjust accordingly.

We shall now go into each of these scenarios in greater detail.

However, for the most part, governments prefer to worry about the youngest end of the population only. It is notable that fifteen- to-twenty-five-year-olds overall score the highest percentage return to work, although it should be noted that the percentage of partial resumption of work herein is relatively high. But the most striking is the very low percentage of work resumptions of over-fifty-fives. This group scores significantly worse than all other age groups. I won't bother you with statistics. Are you aged over fifty-five and you lost your job? Then it will take probably many months to find a new job. It is easier said than done, but prepare for that. See also the chapter about the financial consequences of being unemployed.

In other words, if you're fifty-five or older, you'd better do everything to maintain your current job because otherwise it is extremely likely that you will not find another one that easily, unless you go unconventional. After a long period of unemployment, it is almost impossible to go back to the job ladder. So why does the government not plunge wholeheartedly into the fifty-fives group instead of the fifteen- to-twenty-five-year-olds supported on all sides? The reason is simple. The unemployment rate of the fifteen-to-twenty-five-year-olds in most countries is higher, and the electorate, influenced by the media, demands that more is done for the youth, rather than the silver unemployed. However, the greatest pain is experienced not by the youngest cohort, but by the oldest. There is also an economic component. If we can assume that the working fifty-fives on average have a much higher disposable income than those aged under twenty-five, then a longer duration of unemployment could be more harmful to all. But yes, these are all considerations that are much more complicated to explain to an uninterested electorate. High unemployment, mobs of youths hurling stones and all that, now there is where you can score points. It is, as ever, the sound bite, not the underlying problem.

The big question

The big question is really a simple one. When you have lost a job at the age of fifty or over, think in terms of the heart (rather than the mind) first. Once you have evaluated all your outgoings, identify what is necessary and remove from your life all that is superfluous (and this may even include friends or relationships!). You can be free to start again on a brand new career path, or, if you prefer, you can just focus on what you really, really like. After all, you have probably paid thirty years or so of taxes already. We are not suggesting you become a sponger, but you can still be independent and enjoy life, while you still have the energy and vitality. If this thought bothers you, think that, inevitably, as our physical performance deteriorates you may eventually become a burden to society, but if you led a more fulfilled life, chances of this may be reduced, so investing in your own personal enjoyment can be a good investment for the rest of society too.

STARTING A NEW LIFE - ABROAD

As a race we have it in our genes to wander around. Whether for survival or for economic reasons, we have moved around a fair bit in the history of humanity, and we continue to do so. The latter part of the last century saw the start of an even greater trend in that direction. The free movement of goods was soon accompanied by the free movement of people in search of labour (these are the two pillars of the European Union, by the way). There is now a great flow of people moving from one continent to another - a trend that will accelerate further this century as production models are moving ever closer to an integrated globalised economy. Whatever temporary barriers governments may try to put in place to stave off the flow of people, these will just be palliatives; the only real blocker would be a drastic economic change of direction, but this is something no government is willingly contemplating. However, we are not here to talk about macroeconomics, but about how you could start a new career abroad.

In this chapter we will firstly assume that you are considering moving to another country just because you are seeking employment opportunities and not due to circumstances beyond your control, such as war or similar, or escaping from the taxman or partner!

You are going to carry a lot of baggage...

Let us be clear, we are not talking about clothes or your hairdryer or laptop, but your emotional and intellectual load instead. These two items can be very bulky and will determine the success or failure of the operation.

...Just work!

Removing yourself to another country requires flexibility and a great deal of pragmatism, aside, of course, from a lot of preparation.

Education and skills
Even before we consider the emotional side of things, you need to think about your education and skills. These need to be transferable. Unless you are an artist or an inventor, you would rely on all your formal qualifications. If your qualifications are not transferable you would need to start from scratch. There may be times in life (perhaps when you are very young) when you wouldn't mind that, or maybe your new life does not require your old skills and qualifications, but these examples are, for the most part, exceptions, and in any event they are more closely related to a hard reboot than a soft restart. Embassies and consulates should be your first port of call for this kind of information.

Language
The second aspect you need to consider is language. Unless you are travelling to a place where they speak the same language, you are in for some work. Attitude to languages varies from person to person. Some take to it like the proverbial duck to water. For others it's harder. You also need to think about use of language. If you are a scientist or a mathematician, you already have your own 'language', and it may well be that you don't need the same levels of proficiency in a foreign language that would be required in a customer service job. It seems almost too obvious to point out, but you'd be surprised how many

people travel to another country without a single word of a language and how much slower their integration is then going to be as a result.

Then of course, there is culture. Working in a country isn't the same as travelling for pleasure. You are going to mix with natives, and you are naturally expected to integrate. You may not accept their ways, but you will need to understand them and respect them. After all, you are merely a guest. If the culture is very jarring, unless your job takes you to expat compounds, you need to give sufficient thought to this aspect too.

Emotional journey

Regardless of that entire intellectual load, your emotional baggage will always stay with you. So if you carry a heavy emotional burden, please think long and hard about your true motives behind your relocation abroad. It doesn't matter how far you are going to travel or how different the environment is going to be. Your emotions will stay with you. Initially it may not appear to be so, but if there are deep underlying causes to your unhappiness, these will resurface. Tackle them at the source, then move abroad.

On the same level, you also need to think long and hard about the people you leave behind. You can't take your extended family or friends with you. If you are moving relatively close to home this may not be such a big deal, but if you are contemplating an antipodean move, the sense of isolation and loss can be very severe, especially in the beginning. Strength of character and determination are absolutely essential, and many long haul moves have turned to setbacks simply because these obvious facts of life have been ignored. On the other hand you may be a very independent, outgoing, and self-fulfilled individual. Well, great! You are probably most suited for a long-distance relocation as you will not feel the detachment as acutely as more sensitive souls.

We can't offer you a checklist. You will need to explore your emotions, weigh the ins and outs and all the pros and cons. If you are so emotionally attached to a place or persons and are contemplating a long-distance move try going away for a long weekend first somewhere remote in your own country. Don't even take your smart phone (or switch it off) and get some basic accommodation too, compelling you to meet people and eat out. If you feel uncomfortable in your own country, how much more difficult could it be somewhere else? This is, of course, an empirical exercise, but it may be a valuable lesson.

Stars in your eyes? Unpick them...
The worst mistake some people make is to visit a country while on holiday, falling in love with the place, and then deciding that on the back of those few weeks they would start a new life there. If this is your main incentive to move, we suggest you take yourself off for a long jog, followed by a very cold shower first and a very good look at your life. If you can't find good answers and your dream holiday continues to be the sole incentive for moving, don't bother reading any further as this book wasn't meant for you. Sorry to sound harsh, but when you are actually living and working somewhere else, you have to contend with the

vagaries of a daily routine from commuting to work to buying food, cleaning, socialising, paying bills, and so on. You don't have a holiday rep to refer to and you are probably far less likely to visit tourist destinations in the middle of your working week. Reality soon hits you. If you are emotionally prepared it will be a positive and empowering experience. If your main motivation has been to escape to a tropical idyll without much thought for anything else, you are likely to be much worse off than before.

Preparation is key

So from now on we assume that you have done due diligence, have identified your motives, removed those big stars from your eyes, and are, above all, in full knowledge that this move isn't to escape from yourself, but to build a new and meaningful working life. But where do you start? There are essentially two routes to relocation. One is based on going where your skills are needed. You can find information on lots of websites or even embassies. Several countries are short of specific skills and some offer decent relocation packages, including, of course, a visa. This should be your first port of call. Visa requirements are essential. In economic areas like the EU, resident permits aren't required, but going to a country on the back of tourist visas and expecting to find well-remunerated and secure work is a road to almost certain failure. So due diligence on this aspect is required. Ultimately if you just Google "working abroad" you will access countless articles on personal experiences, guides, and more. Beware, though,

...Just work!

of agencies that offer you to find job for a fee - nine times out of ten they are just after your money.

The other route to overseas relocation is the presence of family or friends. If you have either of these, consider yourself lucky as you will have a soft landing in the chosen destination as they would have prepared the ground for you. You may even have ready accommodation or a job in the family firm! This kind of relocation abroad is obviously the easiest one to achieve. At this level you'll really only have your emotional baggage to contend with, and it will be a balance between what you have left behind and what you are likely to get.

The other areas of preparation have been highlighted in the paragraph above but can be summarised as follows:

- Skills and education transferability
- Language and culture
- Practicalities (accommodation, transport, money, communications, etc.)
- YOU

Working abroad could be one of the best steps you'll ever take, but just like in all high-risk operations, due diligence is required to ensure its success.

Job seeking in Australia
by Peter Ambrose

Setting the stage

The year is 1985, well before the wide use by the population of the Internet. Most job vacancies are placed in the job classified section of various newspapers local and national, or for the more senior roles, display advertisements in the general news sections of state and national newspapers.

Typically, handwritten cover letters were submitted with typed resumes in applying for the advertised position. Recruitment agencies, both large and small, were plentiful and were engaged particularly by mid to large companies to create and place these advertisements; screen, assess, and interview candidates of interest prior to providing a shortlist of three to four candidates to meet the employing client. All quite straightforward really. Like so many other areas of our lives.....retail purchasing, advertising, betting, entertainment, staying in touch with friends and family......it all changed dramatically as the Internet immersed itself in our lives.

More recent times......the pervasive Internet

The utilisation of online resources now plays a major role in the connecting and matching people looking for their next role, to agencies and employers. Advertising by agencies and employers has an important place in attracting candidates. In Australia this primarily occurs through –

...Just work!

- Job boards such as SEEK have wide reach to candidates both by alerting candidates to particular vacancies in categories and locations that they have registered their interest in, or by candidates interrogating job boards for roles they are interested in. Job boards have taken a significant market share of job advertising from newspapers. There are also many specialised (e.g. industry-specific) job boards, which some candidates with particular skills and knowledge may favour.

- Whilst newspapers have seen a dramatic decline in job advertising revenue, newspapers are still utilised by agencies and employers, with the advantage of potentially attracting candidates who might not be necessarily looking for a change of employment. The disadvantage of newspaper advertising, in particular display advertisements, is cost. A display ad in a high-circulation newspaper (say 6 cm x 6 cm in size) can be up to AUD $10,000 compared to an ad placed on SEEK for $250.

- Industry publications still enjoy a reasonable level of print advertising for positions.
- Virtually all companies have their own websites, and many (particularly large organisations) carry a Careers Centre link within the website. The success of these Careers Centre links in attracting quality candidates to an employer is debatable. Still, for candidates keen to join a certain company, they can

be a useful tool.

- There is increasing use of job-seeking Metasearch engines used by candidates. A Metasearch engine is a search tool that uses other search engines' data to produce their own results from the Internet. These engines search job boards, company websites, and recruitment agency websites, often utilising keywords, to aggregate the search result for the candidate. Social media is playing an expanding role in recruitment.

- LinkedIn is being increasingly used by companies and recruiters to 1) advertise vacancies and 2) search for targeted candidates with particular skills and experience.

- Facebook and Twitter are used to a lesser extent but can be useful in directing candidates to vacancies advertised elsewhere or in researching additional information about a particular candidate. Be careful what you put on your Facebook wall.

- Google searches are widely used by candidates to research information about a particular company or industry. Similarly Google searches may be used by agencies or employers to extract public information on candidates.

- Many useful tools can be sourced on the Internet, including resume formatting and tips and interview techniques.

- Social media and Internet interrogation are very powerful methods being increasingly utilised. However, they must be treated with respect to the person's right to privacy. More work needs to be done on establishing guidelines in this regard.

The Internet has underpinned an increase in some sectors for companies to place their own advertisements for job vacancies, due to the ease of listing on job boards such as SEEK. This has seen some work removed from recruitment agencies. However, there are some ramifications for this trend. Whereby fifteen years ago even large companies may have only had an HR manager and, say, an assistant, today human resources departments have exploded in size in many companies. HR likes to maintain control of the recruitment process, often diminishing (sometimes ignoring) the involvement of the hiring (e.g. line) manager. This can have significant downside in ensuring the right match is made. Part of the reason for the expansion of HR departments is the higher level of requirements in areas such as compliance, OH&S, Workcover, training, and so on. The total focus on a recruitment assignment sometimes suffers. A recruitment agent, on the other hand, will usually provide that focus in spades.

"Headhunting"

Recruitment agencies usually play the prime role when an executive search is required. An executive search is engaged typically when a person of very tight or specialised skills, deep industry experience, or unique attributes is required. Also, search assignments are often undertaken when there are sensitivities or confidentialities involved. Research is undertaken by the agency through people and industry networks, personal communication, publications, and of course, the Internet. LinkedIn is an obvious search tool, so candidates should ensure their profile is professional and current and that keywords for selection are optimised and included.

Applying for a job

One norm still remains....the importance of the "Resume". This is such an important personal document that I am constantly bewildered at the poor quality of so many resumes. In any assignment I receive too great a proportion of resumes with spelling and grammar mistakes, poor formatting and layout, inadequate role information. Many of these applications are simply handicapped out of consideration from the first click.

Similarly, in all my job advertisements I ask for a cover letter to be attached addressing our requirements as listed in the advertisement. Probably 40% of applicants fail to supply a cover letter, let alone one with requested content. The only conclusion is that these candidates are lazy or have no eye for detail. It is the easiest thing in the world to click, attach, and send a resume to an agency or employer.....more is required from candidates to establish their genuine interest in the role. I generally find candidates who call and enquire about a role with relevant and sensible questions more often than not fall into the "Look at carefully" basket.

Recruitment tool - testing

Psychometric testing of candidates, e.g. abstract reasoning, critical thinking, numerical ability, literacy aptitude, continues to be insisted upon by some companies and ignored by others. There is no doubt these tests can be useful in identifying a candidate's flaws, weaknesses, and strengths. However, they should always be used as one part of the recruitment process and not necessarily a "showstopper". The identification of a weakness can be turned into a strength with the right coaching and support.

Medical check

Major companies as a rule require a medical check for a variety of reasons, such as future

Workcover compensation claims or evidence of drug use.

Reference checking

Reference checking is insisted upon by almost every Australian company large and small. It is also an aspect of a candidate's job-seeking endeavours that is overlooked in importance. Reference checking is either done by the recruitment agency, the prospective employer, or an independent reference-checking consultancy.

Candidates often provide outdated contact/information details for the referee. They often do not advise the referee of an impending call or inform them of the job in question. It is not good for the checker to call and be met with surprise by the referee. This, again, is just laziness on the part of the candidate. The extent of checking varies. It always will include a discussion on the candidate's role, responsibilities, and performance. However, they may also check dates of tenure against the resume, police checks, and driving record. Again, the importance of accuracy in the resume......missing a date by even one month can sow seeds of doubt in the recruiter's or employer's mind.

Australian Trends

Australia is a large country geographically. However, the vast majority of the population inhabits the coastal fringe, mainly on the east coast of Australia. Not surprisingly most job vacancies are in this region, and even then mainly in the large cities, e.g. Sydney and Melbourne, or larger regional cities such as Newcastle. However, mining and resources (and agriculture) are very important industries for Australia historically and in the future. These industries often require people to be located in remote areas. These jobs are often difficult to fill and tend to pay higher rates to compensate for the location.

As we move into the twenty-first century industry sectors. Australia has built its wealth on mining and resources, manufacturing, agriculture, and livestock. Labour, marketing, and technology forces are now acting to shift Australia's industry emphases. Health and education, technology specialities such as medical devices and agricultural developments are now emerging as more significant industries in Australia, which will translate to jobs growth in these sectors. Construction will continue to be a key sector in Australia, and with significant infrastructure projects on the drawing board, this sector will continue to require skilled people.

The other consequence of this industry growth shift is that Australia is shifting towards industries requiring a high level of education and training, as well as a diminishing blue-collar workforce (also due to technology innovations replacing or reducing required labour input).

No doubt a proportion of the people to help drive the growth industries will come from overseas. Australia is, by and large, a welcoming country for people with skills and abilities to help drive Australia's growth.

Peter Ambrose

A US perspective on job hunting in the twenty-first century

by Evan M. Parris

From seeker to hunter gatherer

This isn't your daddy's job climate. Employment trends have changed as much over the last couple of decades as employment practices and job search methods have. It's no longer acceptable or practical to passively look for a new job. You must be proactive, engaged, motivated, driven, and confident. You must be a *hunter*.

In the past, people who looked for work were often referred to as "job seekers," a term that implies that they're doing nothing more than looking around, scouting the employment landscape for opportunities, and throwing their hat in whichever ones have some degree of appeal to them. And in the past, that may have worked. However, many companies became inundated with stacks of resumes and curricula vitae (CVs) from hundreds or thousands of applicants when maybe only a handful of positions were actually available. When those employers' human resources teams had large staffs and several recruiters to look through them all, it was a daunting task, but not an impossible one. The candidates whose skills and assets stood out from the rest would rise to the top and put them square in the sights of hiring managers.

Advances in technology, economic upheavals, and shifts in

employment attitudes have changed the game in a big way though. HR departments are cost centers, so when a reduction in staff size or budget is needed, recruitment efforts are often the first to go, and so they were. Teams of recruiters were pared down to maybe one or two people – or none if managers felt like they could go it alone. A discerning eye for experience and abilities became a computer-based assessment, programmed with algorithms that weigh an individual candidate's intelligence for value to the company as well as "keyword search" features that parse resumes for only the most relevant details. Where once a recruiter may have reviewed dozens of applications a day for people worthy of an interview, today they only look at a few.

As the hiring behavior for employers has changed, so, too, has the behavior of job hunters. Anyone over the age of thirty is familiar with the old methods of looking for work: browse online job boards and newspaper classified ads for job openings, create a resume, write a cover letter, print it on some nice paper, and then mail it to human resource departments or drop it off in person. Occasionally, you might have been able to get away with faxing or even emailing it to an employer. Then you waited by the phone for a recruiter to call. Sometimes it would take a few days, and sometimes you never heard from them at all. Repeat ad nauseam.

I'm sure just about everyone has seen how things have evolved since then, except for perhaps older workers and senior-level executives who have devoted a decade or more to one company before suddenly finding themselves in "layoff limbo" without a clear idea of what to do to find that next job. Those are the folks who may need direction, but they aren't the only ones. Young people fresh out of high school or a four-year university have also found it tough to break into their chosen fields of study because of a lack of real-world experience and a saturated market of others in their same situation. So how do those groups set themselves apart from the pack? By adapting modern search methods to become skilled job hunters.

Gone for the most part are the days of perusing newspaper classifieds and walking into a business to request a paper application. In the digital age, most everything is done online. From finding job leads to submitting applications to connecting with employment professionals who can move the process along, everything has become dependent upon technology to make it happen. And for mature workers, that can sometimes mean a generational gap when it comes to adjusting to the latest and greatest job search tools. Fortunately, there are many ways for them to overcome that challenge thanks to free classes at local libraries, state career centers, and community colleges, but it still only brings people up to speed with technology. There's still much more involved with job hunting in today's world.

...Just work!

Network, network, network

People who have been looking for work long enough have heard the same refrain over and over: "Network, network, network!" It may sound cliché or overstated, but I assure you that it's not. In fact, networking has quickly become the most reliable method to finding mid-level positions and above in the twenty-first-century job market. However, the idea of networking scares a lot of people because it sounds more intimidating than it is. Networking doesn't have to be some fancy skill that takes years to master. We each do it every day with neighbors, clergy, teachers, friends, and family members, but we often don't realize how effective it can be when looking for a job. The people we know have varying degrees of influence with other people they know, and the people they know have connections to many others as well. If you think about the relationships that you've built with the people you know and are introduced to, keep in mind that they are critical elements of the companies for which they work, and by getting to know them, you're also building relationships with their companies.

The popular professional website LinkedIn works much the same way. By building your network of current and former co-workers, managers, friends, colleagues, and other acquaintances, you can potentially reach thousands of representatives from different companies who may either have open positions with their places of business or may know someone else who does. And although LinkedIn is the most widely used social media tool when it comes to hunting for jobs, it's not the only one out there. Facebook,

Twitter, Orkut, Qzone, and VKontakte are just some of the ones throughout the world with a multitude of users, and job hunters have been known to make as much (or as little) use of them as they choose by thinking of their lists of friends as a professional network instead of just a social circle.

As vital as networking is to a productive job search, the importance of a good resume or CV cannot be ruled out. Recruiters and hiring managers still rely on them, whether they're printed on paper or solely exist in electronic form. However, the typical content and structure of a resume has changed significantly in the last several years. It's rare today that you'll see a resume with a clearly stated "objective" at the top under a person's name and contact information. Not only are resume objectives obsolete, but they suggest to employers that your working relationship with them is more important for what you get out of it rather than what you can contribute to their business. Your resume should never be a tool used to convince an employer to sell itself to you; it should sell yourself to the employer. Instead of stating what your objective is, tell companies what you can do for them by creating a functional resume that highlights your applicable skills or summarizes your background and accomplishments from previous positions. You'll want to keep a list of your recent experience, education, and other related activities on there, of course, but refer to the job description for the position to make all the information as relevant as possible. Instead of attaching a cover letter tailored to the job and the company to which you're applying, which is still perfectly acceptable, you should also make sure your resume or CV is customized for each position as well. Naturally, ensure that any documentation you provide to an employer is free from typos, spelling errors, punctuation mistakes, and poor grammar. If possible, have someone with a great eye for details review it with you.

USA favorite tools

We'll get into some more tools of the trade later, but that should provide you with an overview of how to begin hunting for jobs in today's world. Knowing how to look for them and knowing where to *find* them are two different things though. Increasingly in the United States, most open positions are never advertised or publicized. You may see the occasional large company put out a public notice saying that they're hiring, but everyone will be applying for those jobs and very few of them will ever actually be considered for employment. Instead, focus on small-to-midsize businesses that are in a growth process, but may not have the money or prominence to promote their job openings. Often, an executive or upper-level manager will ask their current employees to refer someone they know before they ever think of looking externally by placing advertisements or contacting employment agencies. That's why an ever-growing network is so important. The more people you know, the more likely you are to hear about these non-publicized openings.

Also consider the type of company you want to work for. Are you restricted by your skills and interests to only a specific field or a small number of companies, or can you be open to many types of employers, including some that you may never have considered before? O*NET Online, a resource provided by the U.S. Department of Labor, provides job hunters with a regularly updated job outlook that lists the fastest-growing industries in the United States and the ones with the most job openings as well as industries that have seen a decline and are expected to trend downward for the foreseeable future. As recently as 2014, the fastest-growing fields have included health care (including in-home care), industrial trades like metalworking and carpentry, information technology/system security and software development, retail and order fulfillment, food and beverage services, and call center-based customer service.

Go after medium/small fish

Because many companies in those industries are still growing to meet the demands of consumers and businesses, they're perfect targets for the hunt. Many include small- to-mid-size employers who are either experiencing an increase in revenue or whose earnings are remaining steady. Along with new LLCs and sole proprietorships, those are where a lot of the jobs will be, and not just positions that make up a bulk of their workforce. Hospitals still need accountants and administrative assistants. Call centers may need chefs or baristas to feed their teams. And several corporations now outsource infrequent needs and more menial tasks to third-party vendors--things like janitorial cleaning, property security, courier services, and even staffing services.

...Just work!

However, if they have opportunities that may be a fit for the type of work you seek, they're still not likely to come to you. You will have to go to them and find a way in the door through traditional and unconventional means.

The biggest key to understanding how businesses approach hiring at any given time is to know if we're in an "applicants' market" or an "employers' market." An applicants' market is a job climate that benefits job hunters, when there are more available jobs than there are qualified candidates. In this situation, people looking for work are able to more strategically target their job search and apply to more positions at more companies than they would in an employers' market. Meanwhile, employers have to work harder to attract good candidates since they are competing with other businesses for staff. Often, this is done with things like hiring bonuses or other incentives that may not be available with a smaller or weaker applicant pool. Conversely, an employers' market benefits companies and their hiring managers by allowing them to be more discerning and selective with a large pool of qualified candidates that are all fighting over a limited number of job openings.

In those instances, businesses may choose to save money by outsourcing the job of staffing positions. As I mentioned earlier, human resources departments are not revenue-generating sources for corporations, so it can sometimes be financially wise for them to outsource the task of recruiting to external staffing agencies. Since the worldwide economic downturn in the early part of the twenty-first century, this is increasingly becoming more common. So if some human resource departments aren't doing their own recruiting, where are job hunters supposed to go to get their resume or CV in front of executives and hiring managers?

The answer is to reach out directly to those staffing services, especially the ones that specialize in filling positions that match your area of expertise. In the United States, reputable employment agencies are paid by the businesses they serve and do not charge applicants who request their job-matching services, so there is no cost involved in contacting representatives at as many of these agencies as possible. And the more staffing services you have working on your behalf, the more companies your name will reach.

That isn't the only way to reach them, of course. There will always be some companies that have permanent, full-time recruiters on their team, so it still never hurts to contact those businesses directly, either through making cold calls to their human resources representatives, sending emails to appropriate contacts, connecting with their employees through websites like LinkedIn, as well as the tried and true method of networking.

...Just work!

Thinking of moving to the U.S.?

Let's say that the job opportunities that are a match for your skills and interests just aren't showing up where you are. Don't rule out going to where the openings are plentiful, and more job hunters these days have started to consider relocating as an option, especially if they don't have family ties or other obligations that prevent them from moving. That even includes moving overseas to complete an education and subsequently pursue local companies that will hire international workers. The U.S. is currently experiencing an influx of university students from places like India, China, Africa, and the Middle East whose H-1B visas allow them to stay in the country after graduation on the condition that their employer will sponsor them. In an employers' market, this can be difficult since it requires a lot more time and effort on the companies' part as opposed to just hiring a qualified American citizen. Difficult does not mean impossible, though, and more businesses are starting to warm up to the idea of visa sponsorship as the job market continues to swell with highly skilled and highly qualified international workers. A quick Internet search for "companies that sponsor H-1B" should return an up-to-date listing of businesses that have sponsored in the past and are likely to continue doing so in the future. These are typically found in industries that have a lot of specialized positions to fill, such as technology and healthcare.

Now that you know how and where to find jobs, let's discuss some of the tools that successful job hunters use to get a leg up on the competition. I've already mentioned

LinkedIn a few times, but there are many other websites that you can combine to make your application stand out. The first and most accessible are online job boards. Indeed.com leads the pack, followed by CareerBuilder and others that are losing steam from the peak of their popularity a few years ago. Part of the reason so many Americans prefer Indeed is because it saves them time and effort by returning search results from several other mainstream job boards as well as corporate career pages, career services listings from universities, state and national career center postings, and niche sites like technology behemoth Dice.com. Nevertheless, it's still recommended to visit some of those other sites along with LinkedIn, Craigslist, USAjobs.gov, Glassdoor, Salary.com, local and national business journals, and an assortment of others to make sure that your hunt for open positions is as comprehensive as possible.

As you can tell by how today's job-hunting techniques differ so significantly from the traditional job-seeking methods used in the past, the employment landscape is ever-changing, and it's not just limited to the behavior of people looking for work. It's also starting to be reflected more and more in the job culture of the companies that are hiring.

There is social, and 'social'

One ongoing trend is to constantly keep up with generational shifts in work attitudes, and companies that do that are often the most successful. Fading away are the

...Just work!

days when an employee's loyalty to the business was expected, and when work was its own reward. Those expectations still exist to an extent, but a lot of employers now realize that more must be done to attract and retain workers, particularly those from the millennial generation and younger. By and large, employees who were born in the 1980s to 1990s have not grown up with a lot of companies that value individuals as essential to the function of the business. As a result, many of those workers only stay with one employer for about a year or two on average, constantly on the lookout for better opportunities and willing to jump ship whenever they arrive. Employers have taken note of that since it can be costly to terminate, recruit, backfill a position, and train new hires. One way they have begun to put a renewed emphasis on retention is by offering good workers more incentives to stay.

The biggest incentive, as always, is money. But that may not just be in the form of a paycheck. Commissions and bonuses for achieving goals or referring additional employees are becoming more common, as are perks that are unrelated to pay. A big sales point for recruiters is the promise of flexibility and a "work-life balance." In other words, they want to assure their new employees that the work they put in will not diminish or take away from important things in their personal lives like caring for family members, furthering an education, or pursuing social activities. They may offer flexible scheduling or opportunities to work from home now that advances in technology have made it more practical. Some also provide extra training programs and tuition reimbursement for employees that are pursuing a degree related to their professional field. Many employers also try to make the workplace a fun environment by holding regular events like picnics, games, lunches, or other team-building exercises. All of these changes reflect a transition in the United States to a more casual work environment, especially in offices with little face-to-face customer contact, where you may be more likely these days to encounter employees in blue jeans and sneakers rather than pressed trousers or tailored business suits. Even socialization among employees outside the work dynamic is encouraged as long as it's kept professional, and that can include grabbing drinks during happy hour or getting together on the weekend for an event unrelated to work.

A lot of employees are also connected on social media sites, but it's very important for them to also understand how the public actions, comments, and behavior that they choose to share may reflect on themselves as an employee of the company as well as the company as a whole. It's not unheard of for an employer to discipline or fire someone for their social activities outside of work, especially if something they do could potentially bring negative consequences upon the business. In the U.S., private companies are completely within their rights to do so thanks to "at-will" agreements in most employment contracts, which permit both employers and employees to sever their relationship without disclosing an official reason to the other party as long as the termination is not discriminatory or if the worker is protected from retaliation such as in cases of sexual harassment or whistleblowing.

...Just work!

For the most part, though, a lot of companies try to be as welcoming as possible and will usually do everything they can to hold on to a good employee once they are hired, which can sometimes make landing a new position feel that much more challenging. However, by using the techniques and methods for successful job hunting that we've discussed, you're more likely to make your own efforts easier, less stressful, and more rewarding than setting your sights on a target without first knowing where to aim.

Evan M Parris

HOW THE HR INDUSTRY REALLY WORKS...

If you want to be found by hiring managers, HR managers, consultants, or headhunters and other sundry recruiters, you have to speak the same language and know what drives them, what kind of tools they use and what you can ask them as a job seeker or learn from them. This longish chapter will aim to give you some understanding on how people in HR think. Bear with us as we think you may find it useful.

Employer branding vs. personal branding

What do we mean by employer branding? There is a lot on this topic on good old Wikipedia, under general branding http://en.wikipedia.org/wiki/Brand or more specifically http://en.wikipedia.org/wiki/Employer_branding

The term "employer brand" denotes what people currently associate with an organisation. Employer branding has been defined as the sum of a company's efforts to communicate to existing and prospective staff what makes it a desirable place to work, and the active management of "a company's image as seen through the eyes of its associates and potential hires". If you Google the term 'employer branding' you will find a lot of information on how companies do their best to show the world what a great place to work they are.

What can you learn as a job seeker from it? You need to show the world what a great employee you are and that is called personal branding. Using Wikipedia once again, we can see that "the practice of submitting a resume as part of their job application process to provide potential employers with access to a number of personal brand assets. Such assets are likely to include a resume, links to a carefully managed LinkedIn profile, and a personal blog, evidence of articles which disseminate original ideas on industry blogs, and evidence of having an online following. Such efforts give job seekers better odds of being noticed by potential employers."

In the light of what we have briefly introduced, we suggest you read more about employer and personal branding on the web, but here is some advice on how you can start with (online) personal branding.

What do your colleagues and prospective co-workers, recruiters, and employers think about you? Every professional has an image as an employee and (amongst other things of course) that determines whether a prospective employer will agree to be in touch. Online personal branding is, for the most part, about the way you look in Google. Are there any photos of you online as a professional? Doesn't matter whether you are a carpenter or an architect.

Blazing hot tips on keywords

We have researched the most well-known (software) systems for recruitment and talent management. An applicant tracking system (ATS) is a software application that enables the electronic handling of recruitment needs. Google the three words *applicant tracking system* and you will find many software companies, suppliers of the recruitment industry. Visited five or ten websites? Have you noticed it is all about *performance, productivity, innovation,* and *learning*? Use these keywords in your application process. Use them in your letter, in your conversations, and on your social media profiles like LinkedIn. How did you perform till now? Were you part of any innovation? Talk the same language. Start writing and talking about your talent and how the organisation you are applying to will need your talent in the coming years. How do you want to be rewarded? With learning possibilities? How effective were you in the past and how effective will you be in the future?

Tracking your profile via social media

Applicant tracking systems have comprehensive social media search engines. They will find you if you use the professional words online they might be looking for. Think as a recruiter. If you were a recruiter, what would you want to know about your candidates before you invited them for a job interview? Some job seekers have nothing online. For full details on how to clean up your act on social media, go to this chapter.

…Just work!

Recruiters see social media as credible recruitment channels. They use a multimedia approach and so should you! Because the bad news is: Not having social media accounts can be detrimental to your job quest. People without social media profiles are viewed as suspicious by *some* recruiters. A multimedia approach will result in the optimum range of *potential* job offers and will ensure you are able to reach as wide an audience as possible.

As in all walks of life, there are obviously exceptions. If you are joining the security services or government, your social media presence will also be scrutinised but more in terms of engagement and quantity. For these jobs normally less is more.

Recruitment events and HR conferences

We have visited countless conferences, seminars, events for the HR experts, some with master classes in recruitment. These are networking events not meant for job seekers but for HR experts and recruiters. Our advice is to check out the conferences and learn who the speakers and influencers are. Then look them up and find out more about the latest trends and strands. You may learn some useful tips right from the horse's mouth.

HR industry blogs

Blogs can help you to be found by the right hiring managers. Take a look what the most important software partners do for the HR industry. These companies are innovative, fast-growing software companies specialized in information extraction, document understanding, web mining, and semantic searching and matching in the human resources sector. Google these four words and you will find them: semantic searching matching software. Semantic matching software also simultaneously searches online for interesting matches on job boards, social media, and other databases.

Consider creating a blog specifically related to your job search, including your resume, samples, your portfolio, and certifications. You can use Weebly or WordPress to make a blog for free. Read blogs of others first before you start your own blog. Include only professional and academic information. Or use your profile on sites like LinkedIn to promote your experience. Recruiters use blogs as a strategic recruiting tool, and you can use this tactic to attract recruiters.

Smarten up your act with search aggregators

The trouble with job boards is that you never know which one to use (that counts for both recruiters and job seekers), and new ones keep popping up on a daily basis. The barriers to entry in this industry are very low, as anyone with some technical knowledge can set up a free open-source job board and start posting positions tomorrow. This makes it more challenging for the job seeker, as you will have to trawl through numerous sites every day, and sometimes you have to sign up and upload a resume to apply as well. By the way, beware of CV publishing sites (these are different from job boards) and under no circumstance upload your CV to those sites with publicly available details, such as telephone number or email, as these could be used by spammers or for the purpose of identity fraud. Protect this information, and if you have no option, get a secondary email address.

There are many aggregators, and one of these is 'Indeed', which collects jobs from a lot of job boards. A company called Recruit is one of the biggest private companies in Japan and bought Indeed for billions of dollars, so that you are aware of how much money there is in the recruitment industry. There are also aggregators for recruiters which consolidate profiles across a multitude of social networking sites. Taking these elements *together* can provide a much clearer and complete picture of who the candidate is. All the captured profiles are joined together and associated with the same person.

The paradox of choice

With so many good candidates and so many CVs, it is not easy to be a recruiter. Suppose you miss the best candidate for the job. It is hard to choose. Recruiters in 2014 still talk about this TED video. It is called the paradox of choice.

You can easily find it on YouTube.

It is really difficult for recruiters to make choices with so many options to choose from. It's more difficult for a recruiter to be fully satisfied that they offered the best possible candidates - there is simply too much going around.

The selection process

Only the best three candidates will be invited for a job interview, and only one will get a job. Applying for a job has become as competitive as top sports. There is only one winner, and being a finalist just doesn't do it. How can you influence the process when the application process is still running? Preparation is key.

How do recruiters select?

When recruiters receive an assignment from an employer to fill a vacancy, they will first look in their own database or in the CV database of a job board, LinkedIn, on other social media, and they will Google. For job seekers with a profile and CV on a job board or LinkedIn, it is crucial to use the right words for that match. Be as specific as possible. Craft yourself as a specialist. This will get you higher in the search results, and it will get more attention of recruiters and hiring managers.

If a recruiter searches for an account manager for water purification laboratory equipment there are obviously fewer search results to choose from than, for example, looking for a project manager. Recruiters look for subject matter experts even for generalist jobs. Your CV title is very important. Only a tiny percent of CVs are read by humans. Again, place yourself in the position of a recruiter. Recruiters skim hundreds of CVs per day. Skimming is a process of speed reading that involves visually searching the sentences of a page for clues to meaning. They speed read and look for certain words about education, skills, work experience, age, and for some, jobs photos.

You have to be in that first batch of CVs which the recruiters use to make a further selection. Suppose a recruiter has selected enough CVs. He will start sending out emails, InMails (LinkedIn), or use the phone to make contact. Picking up the phone and answering the mail will bring your CV on the second stack! Leave your phone ON and make sure the battery is loaded. Always have some paper and a pen ready to write down who is calling you. Don't be afraid to ask for the exact name of the recruiter, the agency he works for, and his phone number to call him back.

Temporary work and agencies

Perhaps you are not ready to find a full-time position or your personal circumstances are unclear. Whatever the reasons, temporary employment may be for you. If this is the case, probably the best option for you is to approach a temporary agency.

Temporary employment agencies, or in short temp agencies, are businesses that specialise in placing candidates in short-term posts.

Employers are willing to pay extra for the services of temp agencies because they don't have to offer a contract to the workers themselves, thus getting maximum flexibility. They also have access to a large number of applicants to choose from and keep costs low in the long run. For short-term or seasonal work, it's usually more convenient to hire a temp worker than to fill a full-time position. The client pays the temp agency and the agency handles the payroll, taking a margin. Temporary jobs from temp agencies are playing an increasingly important role in today's economy. It doesn't matter on which side you are, whether pro or against, temping plays an important role in the total job market. From an employer's perspective, hiring temporary workers can make sense in many circumstances.

For professionals either between jobs or affected by the economic downturn, temping can make sense, and it may even lead to the offer of a full-time post (for which the temping agency would obviously also get a commission).

...Just work!

For the most part, though, many temping jobs are aimed at unskilled workers. Building and agriculture make extensive use of the opportunities offered by hiring workers for short periods of time. Some of the positions may involve hazardous jobs, or those that may not be as popular as others, such as cleaning, for example, or dealing with waste. This is work that has to be done by somebody, though not necessarily by you, of course. A number of these low-skills agencies can even help with visas and education licenses. For the worker, though, any additional facility provided by the agency may come at a price, which would reduce further what can already be a modest income at the best of times.

Regardless of the type of employment or offer, a temping agency can be a good option if you are intending to try a different job. For example, if you decided to go on your own to open a cafe or a restaurant, then spending a few weeks temping for one of those retail outlets may give some excellent insight and may help you make a decision one way or another. You could even network with more senior people in those trades, or suppliers perhaps. At the end of your temping stint you would have probably decided whether the change of direction is for you or not. If the temping is for a short period of time, you may not wish to mention it in your CV if you change your mind about the job, but you would have at least earned some money and gained additional skills and confidence.

Temping can also give you a sense of freedom as, within reason, you are your own boss. That is unless you get too good at your job, in which case you may also run the risk of getting into a temping loop, to meet demand, which may be okay in terms of financial gains (especially if you are a professional) but not so good for long-term planning.

There are thousands of temp agencies in almost every country and hundreds of thousands temp workers go to work every day. Don't be surprised if you step into the office of a temp agency and after you registered there is no job opening for you. You have to pick the right temp agency! There are many specialized agencies in sectors like finance, design, engineers, unskilled workers, airports, and so on.

Look around for only the best and most reputable agencies. There is no point in signing up for those with a reputation which is less than impeccable. So use due diligence, ask around, read reviews on job boards, call them, visit their premises and make an informed choice. Remember, though, that most of these agencies are looking for a specialism so you need to be highlighting a specific skill when you apply for these jobs.

Many will also ask for the sort of paperwork that you are expected to supply to a normal employer, such as proof of residence, ID, health insurance, references, and more. So if this is the route that you would like to take, make sure you have a good portfolio always at the ready.

...Just work!

Finally, when you meet the employment consultant, use the same approach as you would when being interviewed for any job. Be assertive but always be yourself and follow up, but without overdoing it - you don't want to make a nuisance of yourself. You want to be remembered for the good reasons. If you are not contacted or they don't return your calls, just try another agency - it's all about how good the match between you and the agency is.

Career coaches

If you don't know much about the career coaching world, look for a professional career coach association in your country. Are there good coaches and bad coaches? Call members in your region. Check out their websites and their LinkedIn profiles. Also compare hourly rates; some are costly. Many career coaches don't charge for the first appointment, so visit four or five coaches first. Ask what the results will be. If you don't like what your coach is doing after a few sessions, fire them and search for another. Does a coach certification by a career management institute help? It helps a bit, but there are many excellent coaches without a certificate or education.

Why hire a career coach?

With so much self-help around, you may be wondering why you should hire someone else to help. Well, we sincerely hope you may not need to, especially after reading this book, but there are times and situations which may force you to take this approach.

For example, you may resist the idea of putting yourself out there on the web or social media. You suffer from other emotional issues and you prefer to stick to your comfort zone. You may wish a total career change and are unsure whether you have what it takes, or you have been unemployed for a long time and you feel in need of help.

There are hundreds more reasons for hiring a coach. Each person is different and while for some getting someone else to help them would be the last thing they want, for others it's almost a necessity.

Whatever your reason you need to understand that a career coach isn't a counsellor. While some may also be that, if you need help with your emotional or psychological problems, you need to look for appropriate professional support in those areas. First sort out your life, then find meaningful employment. You can't have one without the other.

Finally, remember that a coach will not find a job for you. You will still need to write applications, go for interviews, and so on. No coach will wave the magic wand, however expensive they may be, and land you in the perfect job with no effort on your part. If this is what you think a career coach does, go back to reading your novel. Who knows? With such fervid imagination you may get to write some good fiction yourself.

TOOLS OF THE TRADE
Your own web presence

Think in terms of organising your own campaign to draw in the right companies in your sector and also keep your current employer satisfied, if you have one. You might not have a campaign budget, but as an employee or job seeker you have to realize that a strong personal brand can make all the difference between getting hired and unemployment, or being seen as a an unqualified candidate. Luckily, personal branding can be done cheaply; your own website and social media are the starting points, and it's all for free. Go get the right target audience - recruit your next employer!

When you strengthen your personal brand with word-of-mouth, you can improve your conversion rate of contacts to a successful hire, and maybe also contact a better class of employers. Study 'employer branding' and 'personal branding'. What do you find out to your advantage? What is the goal of your personal campaign? Get rid of unsuitable employers and attract the desired ones? Unqualified employers are going to show up, regardless. Be careful not to downgrade yourself. A personal campaign is about marketing exactly like any other marketing campaign.

The first step is a good website or blog site. Most personal websites are just text, photos, images that will light up your online profile. Try to see it with the eyes of a recruiter. If you were a recruiter and you were looking for you, what would you be looking for?

...Just work!

There may be times when thinking about your personal branding may require external input. In some countries there are organisations providing this kind of advice. For example, in the Netherlands you could knock at Noloc's door, the foundation for professional coaches. There is also an International Coaching Federation. But back to your website. Instead of the dull, dry specs one, you need an attractive and well-designed, short-on-text, and rich-in-info-and-images one. And you need to highlight exactly the features that interest and attract recruiters and employers. The first page can link to the fuller specs on other pages. Special attractions. Every job seeker has something to offer, so figure out what it is for you. If you have a home location, for example, near an industrial area and you are looking for work there, show a map. If you have a beautiful home office and you want to work from home, show your office. Professional challenges: From the employer's perspective, the most interesting, enjoyable, and challenging jobs from the past also tend to have the most career advancement potential. The most important attractions are your colleagues or former colleagues. Professionals and good employers care about the people they work with more than anything else.

Can you create infographics? They are all the rage, and if you could explain in this format either a personal achievement, or even highlight your career path, you are into a winner.

Your website should make it easy to contact you. Don't forget, therefore, to place a contact form on it and to check your email regularly. Your LinkedIn profile can serve to screen them. Start a dialogue with prospective employers on LinkedIn (first study https://help.linkedin.com thoroughly if you are unfamiliar with LinkedIn).

Well-designed personal websites do require a greater investment (in time) than the normal cut-and-paste, so once you've put it together, be sure to get it out on all possible channels.

Referrals are far and away the best way to attract recruiters and employers. Rather than "Hire me," it should be "Let's work together." When social job searching is centered on your prospective employers, they understand that they're not doing you a favor, they are doing themselves a favor by attracting you to work with them.

Your cold email as a job seeker will also get a big boost from a little personal branding color if part of a well-planned personal branding campaign linked to your own website.

Leveraging the power of social media

In this chapter we will be looking at social media and how you can leverage on these channels to get a job or at the very least carry out some research that may help you in your quest for a job.

We don't want to give you an in-depth introduction on social media as there are millions of web pages and

...Just work!

hundreds of books out there on the subject. Our aim is to see how you can use the channels to your own advantage in order to get you to the position you are looking for.

Back to basic

First things first. Do you have a social media presence? If you do please take a few minutes and list all the channels where you are present. Some of you may only have a Facebook account; others may have signed up to countless social media channels. This step is absolutely vital. You must (must!) audit every single one of the channels in which you have a profile. By this we mean that you need to look at your profile from the perspective of someone who is trying to give you a job. So if your Facebook page displays a picture of you throwing up in the gutters after a grand party with friends, while this may be a good indication that you are a fun and gregarious person, it may put prospective employers totally off you. This is, of course, an extreme (though people do put odd selfies online--we know that--even politicians!), but in the more normal case you will need to look at every aspect of your profile, for example:

- all pictures, including those of your friends
- all content you like and all groups you are following
- your friends/followers
- your contact details
- your basic biographical information

We will go into details for each of the main social media channels, but you'll get our drift. You can't proceed to the next step until you have done the basic housekeeping.

All about image

Make sure there are sufficient and correct photos (especially on Google+) of you available online. This has nothing to do with looking good or being handsome. Recruiters want to know your personality a bit more and a photo online helps. Investing in some good photography is essential. Don't scrimp and save, using a supermarket's photo booth, especially on LinkedIn. If possible, if they still fit, wear the same clothes at the interview that you had on the LinkedIn photo - people don't like changes for the most part and they will be reassured by your presence. Recruiters look, also with the help of software tools, for videos of you. Don't put a video of yourself online unless you know exactly what you are doing and have checked this with a professional videographer. Remember it's better to have no video than a wrong one.

Clean up your act first

So here we are giving you a very brief overview of what you can do for each of the main channels in relation to your profile.

Facebook

You can look at your Facebook profile as someone who isn't a friend, and this is the most useful tool at your disposal. Try it out. If there is nothing there that can embarrass your mum you don't need to worry. If you're in doubt, ask your mum (really!) or ask a serious friend (yes, a boring one preferably!). If you have come across some issues, just like the ones mentioned, please take immediate remedial action, hide from public view what should be limited to a few close friends, and so on. When you have done all the housekeeping in question, then repeat the exercise and check again until you are fully satisfied.

We would not recommend closing Facebook off entirely to public view, you can use it to display dexterity in terms of communication and presentation, particularly if your job is in the creative arts, and if you displayed nothing at all you might even make prospective employers suspicious.

Google+
Treat in the same way as Facebook. It's a very similar social media channel, except that some of the functions are different, but you can still see your profile from a public perspective and take remedial action.

YouTube
It's important to remember that while in the past you could sign up to YouTube with an alias, now Google is linking your real name to your own YouTube channel. If you have been on this social media channel for a while, you may wish to take a good look at the way you display yourself, your likes, etc!

LinkedIn
Of all the social media channels this is the most professional (and for some the most boring) as it's, in effect, an online CV and job market... Don't believe anyone who tells you otherwise. Even if people are working for a company, they are ultimately on LinkedIn to show off

and to grab an opportunity if it was ever presented to them. There is some excellent guidance online on how to polish up your LinkedIn profile, and we are not wasting your time here giving it to you again. Take some time to fix, repair, and monitor.

Twitter

You may or may not have a Twitter account, but you will see what is available publicly. Work on the basic profile, your links, and so on, along the same lines as for the profiles just mentioned.

You'll be forgiven for feeling bored at this stage, but this is an essential exercise. After all, if you have a baby you'll have to change its nappies, whether you like it or not. The principle here is just the same….

Sparkling new media presence

You have cleaned up your act and you now have a brand new presence on all the social media channels on which your name is publicly mentioned (have you Googled yourself? Do it now, if you haven't done so already!). You may belong to countless other social media sites under a different name and as long as you don't have anything which is easily identifiable like a picture (or a video) you can rest easily, and you can now move on to the second stage.

The social media channels you have now created and cleaned up are, in effect, your business card. This doesn't mean that you may want to use them all. In fact, we suggest you just use LinkedIn for the purpose of job hunting, maybe

...Just work!

YouTube if you are a creative videographer, and Twitter if you are a witty contributor to some specific field of interest, leaving the others for your friends.

Channel-by-channel action

As you have cleaned up your act, you can now leverage the power of social media to do some research. Essentially you can use social media to research companies and people. Not all companies keep their social media pages fully up-to-date. Some are better than others so you may always want to double check the information you find on social media with their main websites, especially for the latest news. In addition, in the instance of LinkedIn, you may have access to information about their employees and, depending on the subscription level, you may even be able to contact people directly.

For the most part, however, the essence of social media is to find out about individuals, rather than companies, and this is how you will want to use these channels. In the next few paragraphs we shall go back to each of the social media channels above, and more, in order to help you transform them into useful tools for your job quest.

Facebook - to gain intelligence only

Lots of companies, especially consumer brands now, have their own Facebook page. The level of interactivity is variable, but you may only be able to use this channel to gain a more in-depth understanding of a company's outlook, if they have a page that is! We would not advise you to attempt to connect with people on Facebook unless you really knew them. In the worst-case scenario they may block you and report you, or simply ignore you. Facebook profiles, though much abused, are still strictly for people who know each other at a personal level. Just think that in the past you may not even have shared a Facebook friendship with all of your colleagues. So our advice is just to use Facebook exclusively to gain background information.

Twitter - if you must

Follow a company (or a person in a company) if you want to know more about them. Twitter is a good channel, and if you have a good presence, you may even be followed back by the company or individual in question - this may be the start of a long collaboration! Be careful, however, and don't mix messages you're broadcasting on Twitter if you are using this channel professionally.

LinkedIn - your job search companion

We diverge on LinkedIn as one of us detests it with a passion and the other is more benevolent, but we both agree that it's an essential tool for research and introduction. The key is to have a really up-to-date and attractive profile. Don't neglect your photograph, treat your LinkedIn profile as your online CV, request and exchange recommendations and endorsements, and be ready to upload information such as research and other references, comment on appropriate topics, join groups, and contribute liberally and intelligently to them. Dedicate a daily amount of time you spend on LinkedIn.

Some people have asked us whether you would need to get

an enhanced profile (i.e. paid one) or not. This is a difficult point to address. It really depends on how you use LinkedIn, which in turn, depends on the type of industry you are in. If your business area is heavily into this social media tool and you find that you may benefit from using some of the premium features such as InMail, then by all means give it a go, but it's not a cheap option, and there may be other alternatives out there. In any event, a month's trial is often available for you to experiment with it, provided of course, you remember to cancel it if things don't go as well as expected!

Google+

For some industries being on Google+ is a must. For example, if you are in IT or SEO, some of the most vibrant and informative communities are on Google+. Lately Google+ has leveraged even more on its authentication features, so if you are a blogger you can be certified as an author by linking your Google+ profile to your blog. This makes you more authoritative as well as aiding you in terms of search engine optimisation, in some instances. In short, you can leverage this network well if you think it's appropriate. If on the other hand none of your contacts are likely to be on this channel, then you may just want to maintain a minimal presence, putting your resources somewhere else.

Skype

Skype isn't really a social media channel but a communication platform, but one that is much liked by HRs across the world as it's essentially platform-independent (you can run a Mac or an Android system and still be able to communicate with Skype). The beauty of Skype is that you can create as many profiles as you like so you may just wish to create one for the purpose of job hunting with a professional photo and a few lines on yourself (be careful of spammers though). You can then use this channel in the same way as the telephone, except that you may wish to use it for video calls too. We shall spend some time talking about video interviews elsewhere in the book.

Google Hangouts

This is the Google version of Skype, but the difference here is that users are required to be Google users. The system is still in its infancy in comparison to Skype, and while some people are mad keen on it, some are much less so. Google Hangouts is easier to use for video interviews than Skype, and it's also free (group video calls in Skype are a paid feature) but the same video interviews principles apply.

Job boards

Recruitment agencies, temp agencies, and employers can subscribe to a job board with a modest annual outlay of around $2000. For that price a recruiter can search and download all the available CVs, and some national job boards can have more than 100,000 documents of this type.

From a recruiter's perspective searching for the right CV in a job board is like mining for gold, and it requires high levels of knowledge and expertise. Experienced recruiters know how to look only for the freshest CVs. CVs are like eggs - only the freshest do. An old CV, one that hasn't been updated in a while, can mean that you may no longer be available for employment, or that your circumstances have changed. From a jobseeker's perspective we advise you to totally remove your CV from job boards every now and then.

Once removed, upload again perhaps the following day. Do this, for example, once per month, not always on the same day of the week. The more specific you can be in the title of your CV which you are uploading, the better. Don't forget to upload a photo. It is the second thing recruiters look at. Without a photo in your profile, your changes are truly less. Are they looking for beautiful people? No, they just want to see the face behind the CV.

Seconds rather than minutes

A recruiter will only spend a few seconds on your CV. Here are a few tips to increase your chances on job boards. The title of your CV will determine whether your CV gets a first look. A job seeker has to become a bit of an SEO specialist to manage his own CV. Use a simple objective for your profile with only one sentence. Let somebody else proofread your CV; no spelling errors please. Also keep your contact data updated, like phone number and email address. It is sometimes that simple. There are millions of CVs and job seeker profiles online without basic contact details.

The 'right' job only

Suppose you have an academic degree and you have failed to find a position in keeping with your qualifications. You can see hundreds of job postings on a job board and suddenly, for example, a position as sales assistant in a bookstore catches your eye. You think 'no problem, I can do that job'. Yet this could be a mistake. Please don't underestimate jobs only because you have had a 'better' one before! Have you ever put a book in a customer's hand before and sold that book, and what about fast cashiering? Of course, stores hire for attitude and train for skills. There is more to it than just ringing a till, for example, receiving merchandise, identifying, organizing, shelving, and zoning in accordance with store operations and shelving guidelines, and even to lighting.

What we want to say is, don't look for 'easier' jobs if you are rejected for a job which was at your level. If you want a career change, job boards are not the right place to start. Talk to a job coach or a friend who changed his career first. Recruiters or employers behind a job posting are searching and filtering incoming (hundreds) of CVs to make that perfect match. Try to understand the recruitment business and read them always from their perspective. If there is a file on that website about effective strategies to target recruiting efforts, read it.

The more specific your skill set is and the more closely it's matched to the job posting, the greater chance you have of success. If you're not a strong match, it is not worth your time to apply. You also have to get used the fact that there will be no answer if they are not interested. Only apply if your work experience, skills, and education match, and don't forget to include keywords.

One final word. We know that in some countries if you are claiming unemployment benefits, you may be obliged to apply for a certain number of jobs per day, regardless of whether these are suitable or not. Job boards offer you an easy way out of this situation. We are completely against blank targeting for the sake of making up numbers, but we are aware that regulations can be plain silly, so if this is what you need to use a job board for, it's fine too. However, wherever possible, you should use the focussed and targeted approach that we have been advocating throughout this book.

Your CV

The CV has acquired over the last few years almost an air of mystique akin to an old-fashioned book of spells. Countless books have been written on the topic, and a quick Google search on 'write your own CV' returns over forty million articles. Yes, it looks as if everyone has something to say on the topic. So don't expect to find a very long answer in the following paragraphs, but we are focusing instead on *critical* aspect of the CV. If you fancy becoming an expert on the subject, you may have already answered your career's call. Personnel management is definitely for you. For ease of understanding, we have split this chapter into something more like a Q&A section than a conventional book layout.

What your CV should be for

Think about your favourite recipe. It has most of the ingredients you like and it's relatively easy to understand and to turn into a successful dish. This is exactly the way in which you should think about your CV. You have to present yourself so that you can be of appeal to someone who has never met you.

What kind of CV?

There are several types of CVs, but the most widely used are chronological or functional. Each serves a different purpose, and they both have advantages and disadvantages. Generally speaking, if you have just started on a career path (say you have just graduated from university) your career office would have explained to you that it's pretty pointless to write a chronological CV as you would have very little to say - and please don't even think of placing as chronological milestones things like school plays or primary examinations. It simply cuts no ice with a prospective employer. So your best bet in this case is a *functional* CV, one in which you highlight your key areas of expertise and talk about yourself in this context.

Conversely, if you have a reasonably interesting and steady career, a *chronological* CV should suit you fine, provided you haven't changed job several times, in which case please revert to a functional one. A functional one may also be used as an introduction to people who are over fifty as a chronological CV may be too long, but be expected to be asked for a chronological one too.

So is there a rule of thumb? Basically think of your career path as a wavelength. For both extremes use a functional CV, but also use it in your career as a high-frequency footprint, so to speak (lots of changes!). If it's instead a very long-wave one, be satisfied with a chronological one.

Be prepared to have both, though, as in many instances, recruitment consultants, in particular, would have a fixation for a specific format and you may need to supply in the manner of their likings, not yours.

How many pages?
So many people agonize on whether it should have a maximum of two pages or three or more. In truth, it

doesn't matter, and this depends entirely on your career and specialism. For example, if you are an accomplished and well-published researcher, you are perfectly entitled (and expected) to add to your CV a list of articles you have published. This means that your CV could easily run into a dozen pages. On the other hand, if you're applying for a post of receptionist and you have only held two prior posts in a similar profession, a couple of pages may suffice. The golden rule is that it's all about content (information) and presentation. A clear, concise, CV tailor-made for the application in question will be read, regardless of the number of pages. Of course, there are organisations using the number of pages as an excuse to turn people away. We came across human resource offices where someone had ruled out that if the CV came laid out using a serif font, your application would be automatically binned, but these are desperate tactics for places where they receive thousands of applications for a handful of posts, and in reality, when you apply for those posts you are entering a lottery, rather than a professional evaluation of your skills. If you like gambling, therefore, take those applications as such.

Designer or boring?

There is no rule here as it also depends on the job. Are you applying for a conservative profession? Then play it safe. Are you a designer? Then use your design skills to enhance your CV. There are, however, lots of good CV design templates around that are marginally more inspiring than the usual blog standard format. You may wish to experiment with some of them and you just need to Google for inspiration and to download a free template. Beware that you will often have to tweak (or even rewrite) your CV to suit an application. If you select a very complicated template, you may be forced to spend too much time re-editing, and worse, you may screw up the presentation ending up with the proverbial dog's breakfast. So don't be too boring, but also be quite careful. For CVs, the middle path is always the safest one.

Should I go digital?

You can have a website, but most people these days would have a LinkedIn profile (see Social Media section) so you may not need to go to the expense of creating a website, unless you were a web designer or an online specialist, in which case you'd be expected to have a strong online presence, at all levels.

Critical CV elements

Well, some are obvious but you'd be surprised:

1. Your name and contact details
2. A sentence or maximum two describing you
3. Your skills/functions depending on the format you have selected
4. Basic information on previous employment (employer's name, etc.) and job title
5. Your education and any professional organisations relevant to the post in question
6. Your hobbies (but not in great detail)

We have intentionally omitted some content like date of birth, and debates on this point are raging. There are instances in which you may be asked to enter this information, but for the most part a savvy employer would be able to gather the age bracket to which you belong from the information you have supplied them, without having to provide them with the minutest details of your birth place and time, unless you expected to receive a free natal horoscope from them (don't laugh, some less scrupulous organisations have even used this as a selection criteria!).

Should I insert references?
Generally speaking, no. This is an element that is often part of a specific job application and details will be requested as appropriate. References can also be tricky and may open you to criticism - put an insignificant one and you would be derided. Put a very important one and they will run a mile from you.

Should I have a photograph?
No. Unless you have been asked for one, or you're applying for a modelling job.

How many versions?
In an ideal world you will tailor your CV to each application. But we know we don't live in an ideal world, so we would expect you to have at least three to four permutations of your original CV, possibly using a different slant based on key functions of your working life. For example, one more based on a specific skill, then another on a related skill set, and so on. If you are applying for posts in different industries, especially in completely

different areas, say B2B and B2C, then you must absolutely have two versions of your CV (and different permutations for each) as you will be expected to present yourself differently for each of these market segments.

If you have been unemployed for a while and have sent a number of job applications, it's likely you will end up with dozens of slightly different CVs. This may present challenges as you will want to be able to retrieve them easily in order to reuse as appropriate, so please make sure you give them a good name, one that is easy to find in your hard drive or cloud storage, and be careful of how a composite name may look (you'd be surprised how easy it is to create a filename with 'sex' in it... so check this carefully!).

...finally

Recruiters are very persnickety about CVs, but don't blame them; it's your business card and a simple way for them to remove the chaff from the wheat. Be careful, therefore, that you don't provide them with an easy way of eliminating you from the selection process, like spelling mistakes, splotches, and similar horrors. It's always much better to print the CV and re-read, then pass on to someone else, a friend, or someone in the family so that they, too, can check for errors or omissions. Once this has been done and you're confident you have a good product in your hands, you can also be more confident about the next basic ingredient: the cover note.

Another recommendation is about storing those files. If you use online web boards you will be asked to store a copy of your CV with them. We'll talk about job boards later on, but you will need to be disciplined about the documents you upload in them, and if you are uncertain about the boards be careful when it comes to your personal details.

In any event we recommend you store your CV in the cloud, somewhere like Dropbox, or Google Docs, or similar, so that if you came across something while you were travelling, you wouldn't need to be in agony until your return home but could apply from wherever you'd be.

Finally... revise, review, and maintain your CV continuously.

...Just work!

The cover note

If you are not applying in person, you will almost certainly be sending your application in writing. In days gone by, you would have posted the application. Now you'll be emailing the details, or even enter the information in the form of attachments to an online jobs submission site. If you are serious about applying for a specific position, you should be sending a cover note. If you simply press send and all you are giving them is your CV you may as well forget about that post, especially in the current economic climate when you need to be seen as outstanding and unique, and not just one among many.

Even a small note is better than nothing. Of course, we are not dismissing the fact that your application may be perfunctory (say you're only doing it to fulfill a quota for whatever reason), clearly in this specific instance you don't need to spend much time on this point, but then you would probably not be reading this chapter, or this book either as your search for a job would really just be a formality.

We assume, therefore, that you desperately want the job in question. If that is the case, you need to use the cover note or letter to your advantage. Do you remember ever receiving those amazing letters from Reader's Digest? In the UK they were even signed by someone called Tom Champagne. To this day we wonder if he ever existed, and before you rush for your computer or smart phone, we must ask you to let us imagine he really did exist. Please don't break this spell for us even if you knew otherwise. Anyway, this isn't the point. The point is that those were accurately crafted letters. They were designed to make you buy something, to attract your attention to the most salient points (have you noticed that they all include a P.S. with the strongest possible call to action?), and this is exactly what you are trying to achieve with your CV.

You don't need to make it look like Reader's Digest letters, of course, but they need to provide a reader with sufficient enticement to look at your CV in detail, rather than throwing it on top of the huge pile of maybes, or worse, rejects.

Key ingredients

So these are the key elements of the cover note:

1. Make it personal - this may be tricky as often offers are anonymous, but these days with a bit of basic Google wizardry you may be able to find a name or two. We even argue that it doesn't matter that much if the name in question isn't the one of the person who is specifically looking after that job, provided of course, it is a decision maker within the company.
2. Be creative - your opening sentence is vital. Be creative and address one of their concerns (which would have been highlighted in the job advert) from the start.
3. Use bullet points if necessary - they draw attention and can focus on those key ingredients they are looking for.
4. Use the note for information that may not be appropriate to your CV - have you achieved

something that is relevant to the post in question but that may not fit in well with a chronological CV? This is the time to shine.
5. End on a high note.
6. Use good design for the cover note, but please don't try to be too clever. If you know what you are doing and are able to use fonts appropriately, by all means showcase your skills, but we would urge you to be very careful when using 'templates' as for the most part, these are of poor quality, and something which is too jazzy may come across as very unprofessional.
7. Follow your instincts - yes, of course. We assume you have already done some research about the organisation in question. If they are young and informal, don't use legalese. It will not go down well, and the reverse is also true.

So please don't ignore the cover letter. Treat it as a very important tool towards a successful application. At this stage, the note and the CV are the two key tools to help you secure an interview. This is all you want right now.

SELLING PRODUCT "YOU"

Even the most hardened salesman will find himself at a slight loss when looking for a job, despite the fact that the objective of the entire exercise is really to sell your own skills, or to put it crudely, being the product (or service) which now has to be sold. But selling your own skills may not be an easy task. If you're a seasoned salesman with both experience in telesales and in face-to-face lead conversion, then the concepts mentioned in this chapter may sound familiar, but some at least may also provide new insight. The product which has to be sold is you. Think about it for a moment. If your discussion partner in a job interview talks about you, he is talking about what you as a product would bring to the organisation in question. This may sound a little mechanistic--me, a product? Well, it's unlikely that you will find a job for what you are not bringing to an organisation, but for what you can do for them.

Suppose you have worked for years at a car dealership, no matter in what position, then you know by now a lot of showroom visitors always have something to say about that beautifully polished steel which is for sale. There is always something not quite right. For example, the seats are too hard or too soft, the wing mirrors are not the right shape, or the car is just too expensive. It's highly unlikely (though possible) that a customer will walk into a car showroom with a wad of money and a perfect idea of what s/he has to buy without requiring additional sales input.

If you are offering your services to a company, the process

...Just work!

is really quite similar. You will need to develop broad shoulders to take the inevitable criticism during the months or weeks that you are applying for a job. What will they tell you? You have too much experience for the job. You live too far away. We are looking for someone with a different background. And so on.

We start this section with some useful insight from Marcel Elte, personal coach and one of our contributors from The Netherlands.

Your personal value proposition

by Marcel Elte

In business, a value proposition can be defined as an additional value attributed to a product or service that is offered. It is used to create added value to the original product or service. In this article, I am using it to shed light on the added value of an individual person, with or without his or her professional expertise. If you are looking for a job, the personal value proposition is a powerful tool to achieve your goal.

Let me begin by clarifying what I mean by "personal value proposition". The personal value proposition consists of a combination of knowledge, experience and personality, using your own initiative and maintaining your authenticity. Learning how to use these combined qualities is an essential source of power in the pursuit of success. Therefore, when responding to job advertisements, you will have your own personal value proposition if you present your complete self, instead of mainly using your professional or social skills and experience. Using your own combined strengths will definitely increase your chances of success in finding a job, or securing another job or position.

Looking for a job, or changing jobs, does not need to be limited to responding to job ads, or sending unsolicited applications. In the current challenging job market, you will soon be one among many and your chances will be small. If you adopt a proactive approach by showing your own initiative, preparing well and gathering information in advance, you will have much better chances.

Practice has shown that, quite often, organisations or employers have become less and less aware of the advantages offered by a convincing value proposition. Therefore, if you are looking for a job, the trick is to 'seduce' an employer (not in the literal sense, obviously). You should show initiative and take decisive action, with the initial goal of being invited for an interview. Employers are always interested in meeting potential new employees who have something to offer that will benefit their organisation.

Developing a winning value proposition

How could you develop a good proposition that will help you draw attention to yourself by using your specific skills and qualities? Of course, there is no ready answer to that question. However, we can give you some suggestions and examples from practice, which may give food for thought and help you develop your value proposition. The main thing is to get a clear picture of what you have to offer in a work environment in terms of qualities and experience. Then you can start thinking about the angle and approach you wish to take. Below you will find some examples from practice, which illustrate how the use of a value proposition has worked in various organisational environments.

An administrative assistant who had been made redundant because of a reorganisation applied for countless jobs without success. For the sake of privacy, I will call her

Angela. At some point, she decided to take a different approach to finding a paid job than responding to job advertisements. Angela found out who the responsible persons were at the companies she would like to work for. She wrote a letter to these persons. Not an unsolicited application letter, but a chance to get into conversation about an idea, which she wanted to share with a professional. In the letter, Angela described her experiences with the client database of her former employer, which was rather in need of an update. Of course, she did not mention the name of the company. She described the consequences of the fact that a significant portion of the - often sensitive - client information stored in the database was incorrect or out of date. Through the years, information had been added to the client database, while it had hardly been updated. She also mentioned the many irritated responses from the target group, which the company received after sending e-mailings or newsletters. Angela was one of the employees who were supposed to soothe clients and promise corrections after such an e-mailing, in addition to her regular work. There was hardly any time to collect the correct data or clean up the database.

As a result of these experiences and the time-consuming way of working with client databases, she developed a method, after her dismissal, to improve the cleaning-up process of client databases. As a carrot, she hinted at having found a way, by means of regular e-mailings from a client database, to encourage the recipients to check the correctness of the information and provide feedback. In her letter, Angela did not disclose what idea she had come up with. However, she did include a calculation of how much time and money it had cost her previous employer, apart from the loss of client satisfaction. She received an invitation for an interview with the marketing manager of one of the companies she had sent her letter to, so that she could tell her story. The manager saw the advantages of her plan as well as the qualities of this enterprising woman. She received a temporary contract that was later extended because of her commitment and productivity, also in other tasks.

What this illustrates is her initiative, her faith in herself and her added value by turning all this into proactive actions. Furthermore, she remained true to herself in applying the competencies she had to offer.

In many large and established organisations, for instance in the non-profit sector, improvements and changes to how the work is done take place at a slower rate. They practice client-oriented thinking in terms of improving the efficiency of processes, but they do not necessarily make adjustments towards greater client orientation. Below you will find another example. It illustrates how another view on these matters led to a job by using a personal value proposition.

Peter was an inexperienced young man, who was taking a health care training course. He was doing a work placement at a hospital outpatients' clinic. It had been made clear to him that, after completing his training programme, there was little chance of a job. The hospital needed to cut down on costs. It was always very hectic at the outpatients' clinic where Peter was doing his work placement. Because he did not get any real responsibilities, he also kept his eyes open outside the boundaries of his training and work. He had the time to have a reassuring chat with patients in the waiting-room at the clinic. He found that this was greatly appreciated and that he could answer most of the questions about procedures. Peter started to enjoy it more and more. If he did not know an answer, he looked it up or he learned from his more experienced colleagues by listening in on conversations. During this period, he saw how his colleagues at the clinic were often held up by the same questions from concerned patients about procedures and treatments. He started to pay special attention to it and kept a record of how often it occurred. After a period of observing and recording, he made a calculation of the total amount of time his colleagues spent on patients demanding their attention. He calculated the costs of the time his colleagues, who were already working under time pressure, had spent on interruptions. After compiling specific information over a longer period, he draw up a report, which included statistics and cost calculations. He asked for an interview with the Head of the outpatients' clinic. During the interview, he explained his cost calculation and gave a convincing presentation of the contribution he could make to the department after completing his work placement.

The facts he presented were clear and convincing. He stressed that the clinic could even save costs by hiring him, at a modest salary, after completion of his work placement.

...Just work!

Peter was offered a contract which would start after completion of his training programme.

The above example speaks for itself. This trainee's value proposition was well-founded and convincing.

There are many examples of people choosing their own approach. Maybe these success stories have given you an idea of the things you can achieve using your own initiative, contrary to expectations. It just goes to show that presenting your individual value proposition, well-founded and with a creative approach, can be successful.

We can conclude that changes and successful job searches are most effective starting from your own strength instead of outside your own sphere of influence. It is important to take steps and show initiative yourself, if personal changes are required. Government and private employment agencies do their best, but gaining more control over your future is largely in your own hands. And you need to take it into your own hands as well, because finding a job and particularly the job you really want has not been easy in the past few years. However, the tide is turning, slowly but surely. Employers are cautiously hiring again and more people have found jobs after a long period of being unemployed. This is a positive development and it looks like it is going to continue, also because of an ageing workforce. But some things have changed since before the crisis: 'jobs are no longer forever'. Developments in our society and in the labour market are moving fast. As an employee, you need to take responsibility for shaping your own career during your working years and you need to make sure that you retain your value in the labour market.

So it is advisable, in addition to scanning and responding to job ads, to actually take the initiative to 'seduce' employers and convince them of the benefits if you were to be offered a paid job.

It sounds simple, especially to those who have been looking for a job without success for a long time, and have seen their opportunities shrink away. The endless search for vacancies or assignments is discouraging. You should therefore take a different approach than making a responsive offer, i.e. stating the knowledge, experience and competencies that match the request without any hope of success. Try and use a different angle for your value proposition. Anyway, your chances of success, control over your own life and self-confidence will increase as a result, which will also contribute to your motivation and attitude.

One who does not change his ideas, does not think.

Marcel Elte

Distance yourself from criticism

Because you are the product and have to do well during the application process, or rather during the sales process, you have to take a little time to distance yourself from it. You are, after all, a salesperson and product at the same time. The two things obviously cannot be separated, but the whole point of this exercise is to find a workable and constructive way for all the comments you will get. First you need to be selective. If you dare to choose, others will dare to choose you. So hold on to a particular profession or a particular skill. If you are rejected with the comment: "We would have had a job for you if you were a quality manager", don't say you will master this profession with a little effort quickly. However, you can create sufficient room for maneuver. Many professions have a wide field that incorporates more than one perspective. Imagine you are a teacher at a high school, you don't say no to a job interview if there is a trainer, mentor, or coach asked for.

Getting to talk to someone

Back to the sales process. Your aim is to be invited to a job interview. This is your ultimate goal, but in a crowded employment market this can be difficult, so you may wish to focus instead on getting an introductory appointment. In an ideal situation this would be a face-to-face meeting, but these days it's more likely to be over the telephone (or Skype) instead. Introductory appointments are what they are, a tool to get to know each other. There is a chance the organization you have approached has currently no vacancies. But what is a vacancy? Before a vacancy becomes such, it often makes a long way through the organisation. An example. A head of a department sees his team struggling to deliver a certain task. He talks to his manager to persuade him that hiring a new employee would be a benefit for the production department. In succession that manager is going to discuss it with his manager, who tells him that he can submit a request to the HR department. An employee of the HR department will write an internal memo about the job description, do research as to whether or not there is indeed a staff shortage. Now the relevant manager and the head of the HR department will discuss the possible vacancy in the management team. The management team wants, in an entirely different department, to declare two employees redundant, and it seems not a good time to publish a vacancy.

Do you remember we started with the department manager? He still doesn't have the extra employee he needs. Chances are, he thinks, "Wish I knew a good candidate. I would just walk along to the board with him, then they would react quite differently." This is another reason to choose initially for an introductory meeting. Companies receives a lot of cover letters and CVs from candidates they don't know, and those candidates don't know the company or anyone who works at the company. Anyway, they explain in their letter that they would like to work for this particularly company more than anything else. Strange that you want to work for a company where you know no one, where you've never been inside, isn't it? If it is not a well-known company, candidates have never even heard about the company before. Can you imagine that many companies are wondering how sincere these applications are?

...Just work!

If you really need a job urgently and you cannot wait until the right vacancy comes along, then you will really need to contact companies yourself with the objective of seeking an introductory meeting because if you are really interested in the company, they will get you in contact with the right people. They might not have a job immediately, but now you are building your network with the right people. Make a list of company names which can always be supplemented. For example, after a few phone calls the list can be enriched by with the names of contact persons you definitely want to meet.

Creating effective lists

You can create a list by industry, but also create a list by region. A region list is especially useful if you are looking for a position that occurs with many companies, such as accountant, receptionist, salesperson, warehouse employee, or marketing manager. We will now discuss a method used by representatives of temporary employment agencies. By car they drive to a certain pre-defined area, for example, an industrial estate. The representative looks street by street for which companies are suitable for his agency. For example, he lists all the companies that he thinks can use project managers, engineers, or senior workers. This depends on the kind of the employment agency which he is working for. In the morning he will visit twenty or thirty streets. He writes down the names of those companies that are of interest to him. He is not very picky. Such an area can also be scanned through Google Maps. Many industrial companies are mentioned by name on Google Maps, but not all. Back at the office the representative visits the websites of the companies. Especially in the blogs and in the news section of company websites, they will find names and positions of employees. The persons mentioned are not always, or rather rarely, the right contacts for the representative.

Telephone manners

Let's go back to the example of a sales rep. If the rep dials a general number, his aim is to be put through to a particular employee--a human being, not just a voice box. A good rep has nothing to hide. The operator may ask what the purpose of his call is. He will explain he has read an interesting article on the company's website in which the person he asks for is mentioned. If the representative is allowed to talk to the employee he asks for, he will explain they don't know each other. The reason for the call is to change that because he wants to get to know the company a bit better. The phone conversation will be about the information on the website, the company in general, and the representative will find out what are the names of some managers who employ people whom his agency can deliver to the company. The rep will call back in a few days, and based on his enriched list, he now has better contact names as he knows more about the company in question. It is important that s/he is sincere in making contact with that company. The operator at the other end of the line will feel if someone is insincere. Someone who isn't really interested will have little success in making contact.

When cold calling a company, a number of things can happen. The operator explains that she does not see sufficient reason to put you through with the employee the representative asked for. You will then ask whether the operator has another contact person for him. The operator might say that it is company policy not to give any names of employees on the phone.

At this stage you will depend on Linkedin or the Google search engine to find out more about people who work for this company. To find a proper contact takes time, but this is important work.

Some companies have an open culture, and in that case the operator will connect you to anyone you like, even helping you with the search. If the right person is present, there is also the possibility that you may be connected directly to a mobile phone number or will be given an email address. Not all operators, or companies, are the same!

Extrovert or introvert?

You should never call the same company every day. If you attempted again several days later you may even come across a different operator, someone more sympathetic and helpful (though the reverse is also possible too!).

Different people react differently to each other. Sometimes you can connect easily, sometimes not. Remember that your goal is to talk to a decision maker, not to the HR department. After several attempts spanning perhaps two weeks, the right contact person may just be in sight. What now? Hold on to that question a little while. Please note: Some temporary staffing agencies have a bad image. We are not going to discuss that subject here. But don't let that bad image fool you. You can learn a lot of their methods to find work for their temporary workers.

You, as a job seeker, are like your own sales rep, with yourself as staff. We advise you to use these well-proven methods to look for work. It works! All salespeople are first and foremost good listeners, so remember to develop a keen interest in everything to do with the companies you wish to contact. Salespeople tend to be extroverts and professionals. They talk easily over the phone. Do you see yourself as less extrovert or even introvert?

If you don't dare to call companies, at least not in the manner we have described you may be more of an introvert. However, please understand that the principle is the same; you will still need to promote and sell yourself, except that the techniques may change.

… Just work!

Personal reflections on getting that 'perfect' job

by Jorien Stoop

In the spring of 2011, I applied for the position of Project Assistant at a large health care organisation in North-Holland. I had studied Logistics and Economics and worked at a nursing home for my pre-graduation practical training, so it was also health care related. I have always found the combination of 'hard' logistics and the 'soft' health care sector interesting.

My first challenge was to coordinate the move of 60 elderly people to a new residential care facility. The scope ranged from the allocation and furnishing of the apartments to the furnishing of the restaurant. Thanks to well-developed plans, the move was a success and my organisational talents did not go unnoticed.

In April of 2013, I was asked to become Project Leader for the implementation of a new business activity. This was a big challenge, as well as a career boost.

Discreetly, I asked what was in it for me. Unfortunately, due to cost savings, there was no chance of moving to another position, getting a salary raise or doing additional training. It was understandable; these are hard times, what with all the cost-saving measures. However, for me it meant that my development was at a standstill. I decided to keep my eyes open for other challenges. In late December of 2013 I started to approach other companies. I made several attempts - some serious, some a little less serious - to get their attention, yet I failed to be asked for an interview.

In the meantime, I continued to enjoy going to work every day. I was still assigned some important tasks and I felt I was getting better, and so did my manager. He inspired me with his knowledge, business insight and guts. In February 2014 I was offered a permanent contract - a good thing in these times of uncertainty, but I did not get a promotion or a raise.

Turning point

Applying for a job is all about quality, presentation and networking. My first step was to develop my 'online image'. What do potential employers see when they look up my name on Google? The results were meagre. There was not much to find about me. Only a rather unprofessional photo on Facebook and LinkedIn. Working on my online image has increased my self-confidence. Changing my photos, writing blogs about my views on logistics and adding to my LinkedIn account has greatly improved my chances of being found on the Internet.

Networking

Step two is to make sure that people find me interesting enough to look up. This requires networking, without expecting immediate results. Just dropping in for a chat and a cup of coffee. It came easier to me than I thought. For instance, I had coffee with a former employer, I visited the supervisor of a former colleague and I contacted people working for interesting companies through LinkedIn. And suddenly I was in the picture. I had loads of visitors on LinkedIn and family and friends were asking me for business advice.

Breaking the ice

I am not short of guts. But calling a company out of the blue and introducing myself with a view to being invited for an interview was rather daunting. What did I have to lose? Nothing really.

I called companies that had interesting job openings and directed the contact persons to my LinkedIn page. Now we were on the phone and on 'my' platform. I was in the picture, I was on the phone and I gave my arguments for being qualified, briefly and to the point. The conversation was about me instead of the position or the company. This is rather risky, for the employee in question is taken by surprise. Not everyone will appreciate that.

I was invited to send in my CV or motivation letter, or to come for an interview. It worked.

Sealing the deal

For instance, after my call and after sending my motivation letter and CV, I was invited for an interview at a large logistics service provider. During the interview, they told me they had never before been contacted this way and that they were pleasantly surprised. They were looking for refreshing people with energy and guts. Moreover, my motivation letter and CV linked up seamlessly with my phone call. They had rarely met anyone whose letter fitted in so well with their personal presentation. I was invited for a second interview with the Managing Director and Operational Manager. I was able to convince them, as well.

In November 2014, I started as a Project Leader at a logistics service provider. A great job in a fast-moving world, where quality, safety and results are all-important. The organisation pays attention to its employees and is not afraid to make investments. I will be able to achieve personal growth here and contribute to the growth of the organisation. No closed doors, but open and honest communication. This is where I want to be for some time!

Jorien Stoop

...Just work!

THE INTERVIEW PROCESS

Say you have followed all the required steps and you managed to obtain an interview. These days you will be expected to attend at least two interviews (sometime even three!). The format of these interviews varies hugely, depending on the sector, the size of the organisation (and therefore the size of their HR department), your field of expertise, and so on.

In some instances (rarely) you may be offered a job after the first interview. This happens more often for smaller organisations, or where your skills may be so special that they just couldn't afford to lose what may be the only candidate they may ever get. If you are in this enviable situation, however, it's unlikely you will be reading this.

The first interview

After the applications have been evaluated, your employer would have shortlisted a set of candidates. This part of the exercise is fairly neutral and more of a tick box exercise. Essentially your application will be matched against the criteria required for the post in question.

If you have been shortlisted you will receive an invitation to attend an interview. The first interview is about getting to know you as a whole person. You will inevitably be asked to go through your CV, explaining especially the parts that may not fit in, and you should expect to be asked the standard probing questions, such as, "Give an example of an accomplishment" - you get our drift. The details of the job interview are beyond the scope of this book, which is intended to be a primer, not a comprehensive guide. If you want to go in depth into the interview problems, there are several excellent books on the topic and lots of online resources too.

Remember that regardless of what you may have written on your CV and application, you need to make a good first impression. Unless you're interviewed by a robot, the interviewer will look at you as another human being. Non-verbal communication is key, and within thirty seconds of your arrival each member of the panel will have an opinion on you - the rest of the process is to demonstrate to themselves that what has been accepted instinctively can be backed up by evidence.

The more resistance you come across, the more likely it is that you just 'do not fit in'. If this is the case and you find yourself in that position, the worst thing to do would be to give up or give in. If inside of you you feel not wanted, use the interview and the interviewer's skills as an opportunity to learn from the process. Ask them awkward and difficult questions about the organisation. For example, ask them if they like their job. Ask them what they think is the best aspect of the organisation they are working for and whether they have felt let down at some stage in their career with them. Turn the tables on them! This can have two effects:

1. You will feel more confident (what have you got to

...Just work!

lose?).
2. You may even surprise them and they may change their minds about you.

Remember you have nothing to lose (unless you wanted to apply again for the same organisation, but it's an unlikely scenario), you don't need to be rude, but the practice could be invaluable and they wouldn't be able to give you a bad reference (beware, though, that if you are too pushy and you have got to the interview from an agency, they may give negative feedback, so always be polite, yet firm).

In addition to the usual face-to-face process, these days video interviews have become popular. As this is a fairly recent development, we thought they deserved their own section.

Live video interviews

Ever Skyped before? Asked for a video interview? If not, install Skype way before your video interview and start practising with friends or a career coach. What you see is what you get. Wear what you would wear if you went to the office to do a job interview. Take care of the background. You can see what the recruiter is also going to see. A wall without decoration is best. Place lamps lower than you are, lighting from down to above will overcome nasty shadows. Also use some indirect light via the wall behind your computer screen. Check out the alignment of the camera. You should make (almost) real eye contact. There are some tools online to tape a Skype call. Taping and evaluating dry runs is the best way to improve your video interview skills. Very important also is the sound quality. Use a modern and light headset or even better an external microphone and audio speakers. What if the Internet connection is down during an interview? Have phone numbers ready and know exactly with who you are in an interview. Watch your body language, sit up straight, and don't forget to smile and engage.

Pre-recorded video interviews

Find out which tools recruiters use by Googling: video recruiting, automated video recruitment, or pre-recorded video interview. Part of the e-recruitment process is a relatively new but rapidly growing approach that allows communicating with applicants by using webcam technology, time- and place-independent. A recent development in this area is the use of pre-recorded, instead of live (Skype), interviews.

Applicants are asked to answer a set of questions that is designed for the specific vacancy they applied for. Answers are recorded using a webcam and sent to the recruiter, who receives a video of the applicant next to the applicant's résumé. This provides a recruiter with an additional source of information, which can be used when decisions are made on whom to invite for a face-to-face interview.

...Just work!

Because it is a relatively new technology, you should try this at home! But, how to practice? Apply for a job with the software companies which make the tools. We are pretty sure they have an online video waiting for you.

What would you do with a million Ping-Pong balls?

Face-to-face or video, you will be asked loads of questions. Seemingly "silly" interview questions can lead to some unexpected reactions from candidates, and they are used to differentiate between candidates. What would you do with a million Ping-Pong balls? They give candidates a chance to demonstrate their creativity and ability to apply logic. If you are applying for a sales job and want to give the balls away for free, that's a different answer than selling these balls. It also gives the recruiter a real chance to see a candidate's personality and how they might fit into the company culture.

Job seekers need to be aware that less conventional interview questions may be asked. The recruiter or hiring manager can, via these kinds of questions, see whether you can perform under pressure. By answering the question, the job seeker gives an insight into his thought process. The recruiters will get a better idea of the values and character of the job seeker.

What to say if a recruiter calls

The best tip is: Please don't fawn the interviewer, but be yourself and ask questions. Who is exactly calling you? For which company is he working (recruiters will not always answer that question, but sometimes they have a good relationship with their client and they will tell you who are they working for). Don't exaggerate, but also don't start the first minute with your weaknesses (some people do).

Expect question like...

Most recruiters will ask a set of common interview questions like the ones below and it's important that you prepare well for those, too. If you Google: most-asked job interview questions you will find many lists of interview questions online.

For the purpose of this section we recommend you skim the questions below. They have intentionally been presented in no particular order to encourage you to stop at those questions for which you feel you may not have a readily available answer. Those are the topics you need to prepare for. Carry out this exercise a few times. You will get better and ultimately you will skim these questions at the same speed, signalling that you are basically ready to tackle even the most demanding interview topic. If one (or more) questions continue to baffle you, write them down and take your time to create a good answer. It may take you a couple of days even. Don't underestimate the power of this exercise.

Why did you apply to our company?

...Just work!

What are the three achievements you are most proud of?

Who are your role models and why?

What motivates you the most in a job?

Why should we have to take you instead of someone else?

What will you achieve in five years? And in ten years?

Why are you looking for a new job?

What is, given your experience, the next logical step in your career?

What job title and job content fits your next career move and to whom do you report?

What is your motivation for this position?

Tell us briefly why we should give you a chance.

What is so far the most important feature in your career and why?

What is your ambition?

Are you successful if you work in a team?

What are the biggest challenges in your work and in your personal life?

Give an example of a project or assignment in which you have worked with others.

What do you do to reach a goal? Give an example.

How does your education and work experience fit in, in this position?

Why did you choose your field of study?

Why did you choose this school or university?

In what activities have you participated alongside your studies?

If you could do it over, would you change anything in your training?

Connect your degree into your qualities.

Were you financially responsible for your education, or a part of it?

Have you worked during your studies, and if so, what kind of features?

What have you learned from your work experience during your studies?

What are you doing to keep abreast of developments in your field?

Which magazines and websites do you read?

Have you ever given presentations to groups? How big were those groups?

What do you know about our organization and our products and services?

...Just work!

Have you ever resigned? Why?

What other jobs do you consider?

What skills have you developed?

Can you give an example of a situation where you had to deal with a deadline?

Can you give an example of a situation where you had to find a solution for your employer?

How do you function in a structured environment?

Can you perform multiple tasks simultaneously?

What would you like to tell about yourself that you haven't told us before?

How persuasive are you?

To what extent do you have management skills?

How do you react in a difficult situation?

Can you show that you are customer-focused?

Can you show that you are entrepreneurial?

What are your business skills?

Can you tell whether you are a specialist or a generalist?

What have you ever achieved that you thought to be impossible first?

In what situation have you used your negotiation skills?

How successful do you find yourself?

What do you try to avoid in your work? Give an example.

What developments do you see as important for the future?

What has recently been the most complicated decision you've made?

Have you ever won from a competitor? What did you do what the other didn't do?

If you look at your resume, can you then in one minute or less tell us why you've changed jobs every time?

What did you like most in your last job? And the least?

What was the hardest part of your previous job?

What was the easiest part of your previous job?

What kind of work do you do now?

Do you have questions for us?

Will you tell us something about yourself?

Would you describe your ideal job and what you value in it?

What are your strongest qualities?

How do you define success?

...Just work!

How do you define failure?

Have you ever experienced a failure? What have you learned from it?

Have you ever had problems with teachers, supervisors, or colleagues and how did you handle it?

What does the term 'work ethic' mean for you and what is your work ethic?

How does your work ethic relate to others?

If there are two management positions for you to choose from, would you pick the 'people' one or the 'project' one and why?

In which direction would you like to develop further?

What type of company is best for you?

What is the best thing you've accomplished in your life until now and why?

If we ask your friends what kind of person you are, what would they tell about you?

What kind of job do you prefer and why?

What would you like to change in yourself and why?

How do you think a former mentor or supervisor would describe your work?

Do you prefer to work under a supervisor or do you prefer to work independently?

What kind of leadership do you like the most?

Do you prefer large or small organizations? Why?

How do you feel about travelling?

How flexible are you in relation to working hours?

What is, for you, the ideal employer?

What is important in your work?

Can you listen?

Are you resourceful? Give an example where it shows.

Have you experienced stress? What did you do?

What are your hobbies?

What would be the ideal vacation at this time for you and why?

Have you ever done volunteer work? What kind?

What do you think about working overtime?

Clothes do make the man, or woman!
by Arnold Fontijn

Presenting yourself well is very important. When you are applying for a job, but also when you want to achieve something in your job. Our clothing is how we package our expertise, knowledge and skills. In communication, seventy percent is about the picture we see. This immediately makes clear how important our clothing is in daily life, in all kinds of areas.

Who can make the difference?
How do you make your mark in the labour market if there is a lot of competition? When you are applying for a job, you need to stand out in a positive way. You are not the only one who badly wants the job. You may be better and have more expertise and knowledge, but these are not the things that make you stand out. If you did, there would have been no need to respond to the ad.

So what is the distinguishing factor? It is you! Yes, it's all about you as a person. What have you got to offer over someone else, that will make the employer choose you? Nowadays, customers no longer choose a company for the product or service it provides, they choose a company for the kind of people who are working there. We probably need not worry about your knowledge. You may have followed several training courses (or devoured this book!) to learn the proper skills and rules of conduct. But what about presenting yourself properly?

Presenting who you really are

You only have one chance of making a first impression. This first impression is really important. It will decide whether someone wants to continue the relationship. A good first impression will increase your goodwill factor, and therefore your chances of a job, and it will make doing business easier.

A first impression is all about appearance. A person's appearance is the first thing you see and the last thing you forget. Just think of someone in your own personal environment whom you have known for a long time and you will probably remember exactly what kind of impression that person made on you when you first met.

When we first meet, we shake hands and, subconsciously, we scan each other from top to toe. And, also subconsciously, we then decide what we think of each other and what direction the conversation will take.

What you wear plays a big part in this. If you want others to believe that you are, for instance, reliable, professional or customer-friendly, you need to emanate these qualities. If your appearance does not match what you are saying, it will be a tough job to get your message across. Make sure you are authentic and true to yourself.

Nowadays, we also see everyone on social media. Make sure your appearance matches your story here, as well.

Exuding confidence

People working in business often wear some kind of business attire. It is not always clear what type of clothing is required, or sometimes even mandatory.

…Just work!

A well-dressed person wears clothes that help you project the proper image and that match:

- the expectations of the potential employer (customer);
- your figure and natural colouring;
- the image of the future employer, the position and the occasion.

Most importantly, your clothing should complement you as a person. If you wear clothes that don't suit you, you feel uncomfortable in them and it will show. If you know you look good, you square your shoulders, raise your chin and you will exude self-confidence. That is what people will notice. It is still true: what looks good, sells better!

Your appearance determines whether you are, and will continue to be, successful and will help you achieve your goals. Not just when you are applying for a job, but also in the longer term.

What you wear is a reflection of your self-image. If you look untidy, dress indifferently, look insecure, this will have a negative impact on how you come across. You will project a negative image to the other person, which will elicit a negative response and may have negative consequences.

If you are impeccably dressed fitting the occasion, this will give you confidence and you will exude competence. You will command respect because of your attitude, personality and clothes. You will project a positive image to the other person, which will elicit a positive response and will have positive consequences.

First impressions

From the moment we see someone, we form an opinion about them. This opinion is based on what we see, clothing, grooming, length, size and attitude. We all do this, even those who say they only want to look at a person's inner self. After all, we don't know the other person yet.

The first impression provides a certain frame of reference when you meet someone for the first time. If you make an untidy or angry impression, you will have difficulty in changing this image. And during a job interview, you do not have the time and opportunity to do that. The decision whether or not to continue with you is taken during the first few seconds.

This probably sounds familiar. When you read a book, you have an image in your head of the characters and what they look like. If the book is turned into a film later and you go to see it, you are sometimes disappointed. Often, the characters are completely different from what you had imagined. As a result, you do not like the film very much.

There is a similar risk in the use of social media. Just think of a LinkedIn profile with a photo and compare it to a character in a book of which you have formed an image in your head. The first meeting is the film. If the image does not match reality, your reaction will be that this is not the right person. You do not like the person and there will not be a next meeting.

A first impression is very powerful. Therefore, you should make sure that you make a good first impression.

…Just work!

Total look

Research has shown that about 50 per cent of the total impression you make is determined by what the other person sees of you: looks, age, style of clothing, posture, facial expression, gestures and eye contact. This means that you can greatly influence the other person's opinion of you by your choice of clothing. What the other person hears: voice, intonation, pitch, accent and pronunciation, accounts for about 35 per cent of the impression you make. That leaves only 10 per cent for what you are actually saying and the contents of your message!

Your clothing gives a certain impression by its style, colour, quality and accessories.

Your outward appearance is determined by:

- the face: skin, teeth, breath, make-up, facial hear;
- the hair: length, style, hairdo, colour, grooming;
- the body: length, weight, body odour, hands, nails.

Therefore, the right colour and style of clothes can give you a headstart. This is how you express your personality. You show who you are and the other person will not get the wrong impression of you.

A suit for every occasion

What clothing is suitable for a job interview? We can distinguish three styles:

- business / representative;
- sporty business / smart casual;
- leisure.

You can decide for yourself what you should wear if you are invited for a job interview. It is advisable to do some research beforehand, so that you know what kind of company you are dealing with. The most important rule is "better overdressed than underdressed".

Business / representative

There is hardly any difference between a professional business look for a man or a woman.

For a man:

- a two-piece or three-piece suit with a long-sleeved, ironed shirt, tie and smart shoes;
- the suit should be made from wool, or a wool blend containing at least 55% wool;
- the suit should have a good fit and should not be too baggy, tight, long or short;
- leather shoes with thin, leather soles, which should be darker in colour than the trousers, and (long) socks that match the colour of trousers or shoes.

For a woman:

- a jacket is an absolute 'must' and can be worn with skirt or trousers (with a crease);
- the suit should be made from wool, or a wool blend containing at least 55% wool;
- wear a blouse underneath the jacket; this looks better and more professional than a t-shirt or turtleneck;
- leather shoes (pumps) with thin, leather soles, which are darker in colour than the suit;
- open-toed shoes are not appropriate, and if you wear a skirt, wear tights, no matter what the temperature is.

...Just work!

Sporty business / smart casual
Also with this style, there is hardly any difference between men and women.

For a man:

- the jacket may have a different colour than the trousers;
- no jacket;
- patches on the elbows;
- shoes with (thick) rubber soles;
- cotton or linen suit.

For a woman:

- the jacket may have a different colour than the trousers;
- no jacket;
- clothes made from cotton, leather or linen;
- open-toed shoes (pumps);
- boots under a skirt.

Leisure
Here is a list of the things that are generally considered leisure wear:

- sleeveless shirts;
- collarless shirts;
- worker jeans
- bra straps showing;
- bare belly;
- jeans;
- low neck.

I hear you say: "Jeans? And what about smart jeans?" But when are jeans considered smart? Should it be dark or light, with or without bleach stains, with or without rips. Some people think that dark jeans are OK, others think they are not. To prevent discussion, jeans are considered suitable only as leisure wear.

Common mistakes

For a man:

- one in every three men wears clothes that do not fit. This will cause you to make an indifferent impression, or can even make you look careless or sloppy;
- to save money, people sometimes choose clothes made from synthetic materials, leisure shoes or polyester ties;
- also, people often think that a separate jacket and trousers look better, sharper and more casual, while suits are old hat. But stylish is quite another thing.

For a woman:

People have different customs depending on where they live. In the Netherlands, for example, women take many liberties in how they dress. They especially make an effort to look smart, young and sexy, which has nothing to do with a professional appearance.

- they sometimes look as if they are going to take the dog out for a walk in the woods;
- they may make no distinction between business and leisure wear;
- they may wear wrong fabrics;

- they often wear tight sweaters and t-shirts instead of blouses and jackets;
- they wear the 'wrong' (i.e. not business-like) combination of footwear, especially boots;
- skirts may be too tight and too short.

Colour, friend or foe?

Colour use and style of clothing play an important part in looking good, making a good appearance and making a good first impression. Colour and style are very important aspects of your total image package. I will discuss the basics to help you find out what your best colours are and what your personal style is.

Colour is an extremely powerful tool. Colours in your clothing can enhance your features, but they can also make you look drab and dull. Wearing the wrong colours will make you look older, more tired, pale, standoffish, hard, unfriendly etcetera, etcetera.. And I think you don't want to look like that at a first meeting. Not then and not ever.

Johannes Itten, who taught at the Bauhaus, was the first to discover 'subjective colour', i.e. everyone has their own personal colour sense. However, there seemed to be a remarkable similarity between facial colouring and the colours used in painted portraits of people.

When we determine suitable colours for our clothing, we start from the three primary colours yellow, red and blue. After all, as everything in nature, the colours of our hair, skin and eyes are made up of these three primary colours.

Depending on hereditary factors, four colour schemes can be distinguished, which match the colours of the seasons. You can be either a spring, summer, autumn or winter type. These are just four general colour types. We have looked further at the colour of hair, eyes and skin and determined that there are twelve different colour types.

Many colours look ok, but some colours just look better and flatter the person wearing them. If you wear the wrong colours you may hear "that's a nice jacket you're wearing". So your clothes are drawing attention instead of you. If you wear the right colours, it's quite a different story. You get comments like "Wow, YOU look great". The clothes do not distract, you get the full attention and your message comes across. In communication, it is all about getting your message across!

Pick the right colour for you
We determine what colour type you are by comparing one colour to other colours, based on a set of rules.

Hair:

We are talking about your natural hair colour, i.e. the colour it had when you were about twenty or so.

The shade of your hair determines the darkness of your colours.

- light blonde to dark blond = light colours
- light brown to middle brown = middle colours
- dark brown to black = dark colours

Eyes:

Eyes can be mix of colours, but two colours are dominant: blue or brown.

If your eyes are blue, grey or green, you look better in blue colours.

If your eyes are brown or green, you look better in brown colours.

It is not just the colour of your eyes that plays a part, it is also the brightness. If your eyes are bright and sparkling, you look better in bright and sparkling colours. If your eyes are somewhat dull and lustreless, you may look better in dull, muted colours.

Skin:

The colour of your skin is determined by the pigments present in it. Our skin is made up of all kinds of combinations of warm and cool pigments. If your skin has more warm pigments, we call it yellow and your undertone is yellow. If your skin has more cool pigments, we call it pink and your undertone will be pink. The colour of your skin is the most difficult to determine. Even if your skin seems yellowish, it does not necessarily mean that you have a warm skin.

The colours that are in harmony with the colours of your hair, eyes and skin are also the favourite colours of your inner self. You can use these colours for decorating your house.

What suits you best

Your style of clothing should not be determined by the social circles you move in, but by what suits you best. In our style advice, we do not use the usual terms apples or pears, or H and A shapes. We look at the round and straight areas of the body. These areas etermine your preferences for forms, materials and lines in clothing.[1]

---

[1] The findings in this section are based on unpublished research

Like with colour types, several style types can be distinguished, varying from straight to more rounded, organic or irregular. When we give a styling advice, we look at the shoulder blades, are they straight or rounded. Do you have a hollow back or not. Do you have round or flat buttocks, slim or fuller thighs. We also look at whether or not you have a waist.

In clothing, we also see these straight and round forms. The straight type likes tight, sturdy, simple, smooth, straight lines, stiff, hard. The round type likes soft, supple, detailed, frilly, loose, relief, round lines, moving, flamboyant, cuddly, wrinkled, stretchy, and floppy.

When you know what style suits your body best, it will make choosing clothes easier and you will be able to look your best. And knowing that your clothes look good on you will make you appear positive and self-assured.

The results of a style advice for clothing can also be applied to your preferences for shapes, materials and lines in your interior and many other areas. If you have a straight body shape, a minimalist decoration with materials such as glass, wood and metal will appeal to you. The straight type likes symmetry and everything is aligned straight. The round type is often a little more messy, chaotic and homey.

You are you own calling card!

Stand out from others by being yourself. Show who you are and look good in clothes that have the colours and style that fit you. A good appearance will work for you, in business as well as socially. You are your own calling card. Be

by Ada Nijman, founder of ImageProof, a market leader on image consultancy.

...Just work!

aware of your appearance and make sure that it is how you want to appear. Consultants like Image- & InterieurProof will help you stand out and create an image that fits your personality. What looks good sells better!

If you have any questions, or if you would like more information or advice you can contact me directly using the details in the contributors' page. Colourful greetings!

Arnold Fontijn

The assessment centre

If you managed to get through the first two hurdles of having your CV accepted and got through the initial interview, and especially if you have either applied for a very large organisation (possibly as a recent graduate) or a post in government, chances are that you may now be asked to attend an assessment centre. We won't spend too long on this topic as there are dozens of books on the subject, as well as quite a lot of information normally provided by anxious career officers at various universities, but will just give you a flavour of the process.

Generally speaking, the assessment centres are a wonderful money-spinning operation for the company that runs them, and at their crudest they are nothing more than an additional filter to make the selection process more manageable when lots of candidates apply for the same post. If you are applying for a job in government, assessment centres are mainly used to select candidates who meet a certain profile, suitable to the specific post and department you may be working for - be prepared to empty your mind and to become pliable and accepting as this is what the tests will try to ascertain. So if you are of the entrepreneurial kind and prefer to think on your feet, these skills (highly prized in some sectors) would be highlighted by the tests and you may be deemed unsuitable for a government post - your application would then reach a dead end. You may be invited for a second interview, which in this case would merely be a debriefing session (more like a justification for the process in question).

...Just work!

Think about your skills and ambitions, therefore, before you accept the offer of an assessment centre.

In any event it is likely that you will be told what tests you will undertake and how the day will pan out (it is often at the very least half a day) - pay attention to the instructions and do some research on the elements mentioned. If you have applied for a job that requires advanced mathematical skills and this isn't your forte, you may want to reassess your application or undertake some training - if you have the time that is. Broadly speaking, there are two sets of tests, one based on role play activities which could be as a group or individual, the other as written exercises. These could be in a variety of formats, multiple choice, essays, an almost infinite set of interpolations. There is no secret recipe for success, and in general terms recent school leavers are at an advantage when undertaking such tests, as they have been trained to answer questions in a specific format. The best advice we can give you is to read all the questions very carefully, taking time replying but working within the allotted schedule and, if possible, without stressing too much (a little stress does help, but too much confuses you).

Other obvious advice applies, like don't go out the previous night on a drinking binge - your intellectual performance will be impaired - and if sick you may be better off negotiating a reassessment day than attempting to sit through the tests with a stomach bug. It's all the usual common sense. Also, do find out about dress code and see that you're appropriately but comfortably dressed. All the other advice that applies to interviews applies to assessment days too (find out about the venue, arrive on time, etc.). We can't offer additional advice that will make this ordeal more bearable. It's just a hurdle that needs to be passed, and to this day we haven't yet come across anyone who has ever mentioned enjoying the process, just like you'll never hear anyone saying that their last visit to the dentist to have a filling seen to was one of the highlights of their year.

Whatever the outcome do not get too hung up about it. Remember, this isn't a life assessment, and it's a virtual given that some of the geniuses of the twentieth century would probably have failed many of these tests. Failing is merely an indication of how badly your beautiful and valuable skills would have fitted into that organisation. So it doesn't make you a less lovable or intelligent individual, it just means that you were applying for the wrong job - they were looking for a sparrow, not an eagle maybe. If you instead pass the assessment, give yourself a huge pat on the back as you have obviously chosen the right job and have demonstrated that you also have what it takes to fit the required organisational criteria. Your final interview in that case is more likely to focus on some of the 'improvement areas' that the tests have highlighted, so do ask for feedback before you attend the following meeting, or you may find yourself at a distinct disadvantage - you're nearly there.

Finally, if you have failed the assessment, unless you have masochistic tendencies we do not recommend perusing the results - remember these are tailored to the post and organisation so trying to read too much into them will not

...Just work!

be a constructive exercise, particularly if you have the tendency to be too self-critical or have been unemployed for a while - one of the key ingredients of finding employment is a positive attitude and anything that may undermine that approach must be discarded at all costs. So if you have failed and they have sent you some feedback material get a few matches, find a safe place, and set it alight, then pour yourself a drink, but think carefully about your next job move. Don't go for a post identical to the one you have just applied for.

A last word, if you are over forty and unless you have been given very clear directions and been told that the assessment is a mere formality, do not bother. You may find the exercise too stressful and none of the valuable skills you have learnt through hard graft (and know they work) would come in handy in a group exercise made up mainly of high-testosterone youths - you deserve better at that stage in life.

The second interview

If you have reached this stage you are likely to be among a shortlist of maximum three to four candidates. Getting to this stage means that you have cleared the basic hurdles (i.e. you are employable, you fit in with the overarching organisational ethos, you have basic job knowledge). You now need to fit in with the team, and above all, your line manager needs to 'like you' and be confident that you will be seen as an asset as this would add kudos to his/her post too.

At this stage of the process interpersonal skills are even more important than at stage 1. You would also be expected to be asked more probing questions about the specific skills required in your job. There may be even instances in which you could be asked to do a presentation or to explain in detail how you would address a specific topic.

Research thoroughly the organisation. With social media you will be able to find a wealth of information about your immediate boss. Use this to your advantage (but don't appear as you have been scouting around for personal information - reminding them of their picture of their dog will not endear you....). Look out for opportunities in the market in which they operate, and without revealing too much, offer them appetisers of your possible approaches and even solutions.

Beware of organisations in which they are asking you to compete for a post by requesting you to produce an answer to highly complex and technical matters. There are unscrupulous companies around who are intent in using the high number of candidates around to gain free knowledge. Believe in your instincts; if you smell a rat you are likely to be right. Your knowledge is what makes you unique and it's where your personal assets are - would you give away your newly acquired smart TV for nothing? Then don't part with what may have taken you years of hard graft to acquire. Tease, but don't give freely.

The thank-you note

So much has been written about the thank-you note....! Should you write, should you not, should you email, who do you send it to if it was a panel interview, and so on.

Rest assured that there are no fixed rules about this point. It all depends on the type of job you are applying for, the organisation, the customs of your specific country, and more.

If you think it is appropriate to send a thank-you note then do so. Be original, but above all be you. The thank-you note is particularly important (and appropriate) if you have omitted something really important - say you had a brainstorming moment on leaving the interview centre. By all means take advantage of electronic communications and drop them a line with your new thoughts. It is unlikely that interviewers will decide on the spot, and it's often the case that the final decision is left until the following day. A thank-you note with some additional information may still sway it in your favour.

However, a lukewarm and simple 'thank you' may not cut any ice, and if you really have nothing else to say, rather than appearing tepid you may as well not bother. Above all, and as we said at the start, follow your own instincts and any knowledge you may have on the organisation in question.

...Just work!

THE JOB OFFER

Intrigued? Why would we want to write about job offers, you may think? Most books on the subject would end at the previous step, but we'd like to go beyond the mere quest for a job. We want you to find fulfilment, not just a job.

If having gone through all the steps, you are offered a job, you continue to be the master of your own destiny. Do not for one single instance think that you have made an irrevocable and binding commitment. If you have any misgivings about the post in question, this is the time to reassess the situation. After all it's much more honourable to decline at this stage, as the second choice might really want that post, than a few weeks down the line when you suddenly find yourself in the wrong company.

Like what they say about writing in haste, do not accept at full speed either. Leave it until the following day, unless of course, it really was the job of your dreams and you desperately want it. The 'digestive' process is particularly apposite if you have any misgivings, however tiny. Take the next few hours off, and then when you get back, write all the pluses and minuses of the post in question. If they equate you may be in trouble... only go for the post if there are more pluses than minuses, but this is a very broad analysis as some of the pluses and minuses may be weighted differently - only you will know.

What we are saying, and what we have been saying all along, is that you need to be fulfilled. This is the time for you to move into the right direction, not just where circumstances may push you.

...Just work!

IN THE END IT'S ALL DOWN TO YOUR IMAGINATION...

So far in this book we have gone through a very comprehensive list of action points. Although we aimed to be innovative, we adhered to the more conventional approach on looking for jobs based essentially on standard presentation tools, research application, marketing, and sales techniques.

With online marketing, however, the possibilities are now limited only by your imagination, though we suspect that if you are reading this book you may be looking for a little bit of help - after all, if you had already got the ideal approach you really wouldn't need any assistance.

So the aim of this brief chapter is to make you think about thinking laterally. In particular, if after applying most of the techniques we have highlighted you are still out of work, rather than making you feel a failure (nobody is!) it may just be that you will need a less conventional approach to job hunting. *Do not despair; the web is your best friend for such an approach.*

There are countless examples online of job opportunities or ideas. You just need to Google this phrase to get an idea. But we particularly like what has now become almost the case study par excellence. We are talking here about Alec Browstein. The guy who got the job he really, really wanted just by spending $6 on Google AdWords. How did he do it? Well, he really followed most of the advice in this book first of all, like doing research, and then all he did is he used his online skill to create a website and specific pages linked to a Google AdWord campaign in which he paid for ads to be pushed when a key account director of the companies for which he wanted to work Googled himself. Please look up his video and spend a couple of minutes viewing it. His approach may not suit everyone. Indeed if you are looking for a job in a more conservative industry, it may be a waste of time, but hey, this guy used his imagination and got where he wanted to be.

Think back about your skills. You may be an excellent photographer, or videographer, or budding writer. Use any of these skills to promote and market yourself. There isn't a single part of you which is ever wasted, so even if your key interest was making puppets out of sourdough, use this talent to promote yourself, well, obviously in the right direction.... but you'll get our drift, we are sure.

Above all:

- Don't make job hunting a chore. Be playful, inventive, and imaginative.
- Be yourself.
- Be professional.
- Be truthful to yourself.

The last point is particularly poignant. If you have had several career changes in your life, you may need to ask yourself the crucial question of why this has happened. It may just be bad luck, but in most cases this may be due to a symptoms of something else. Being truthful to yourself is the best advice we can give anyone. If your job doesn't fulfil you and it becomes a drudgery, you will be out of it sooner or later. You may not consciously want to lose it, but you will, because your deeper self is not satisfied. In some extreme situation you may be able to stick to it, but you may even develop other symptoms like illness or depression. So use unemployment as an opportunity to find the new you, rather than going back to the old one. Challenge yourself, be creative, be imaginative, throw away the rule book, burn this ebook. Have fun and reinvent yourself!

A word about 'positive' thinking

Across this book we have made every attempt to make you feel positive about your personal challenge. Out there, in the wide and wild world of publicity and promotions, you will find lots of books that may appear to offer you a quick fix for all your life situations just by the use of positive thinking, something along the lines of 'think you are wealthy and you will become rich'. Alas, such simplistic approach will seldom work. This isn't because we don't believe in positivity (quite the opposite), but because there are often deep subconscious reasons behind many of our problems. **These underlying issues need to be addressed first.**

If you start bringing positive thought to big and troublesome external circumstances, without first getting to grip with the seemingly small and hidden issues inside you, you will not succeed. In fact, by just thinking positive about an unbearable situation you may even make it worse! This may sound like a paradox at first, yet think of thought as a form of energy, or if you are more comfortable with tangible stuff compare it to something like water. You can't make water run uphill just by desiring it to do so, or by adding more of it to a pond as it will just overrun. But if you get to the bottom of it and engineer systems to address the real problem you can make true progress. Using water as a parallel rather than 'forcing' it uphill with your hands you may wish to get a bucket first, you'll soon think of using a simple water wheel and finally you may be building a fully-fledged pumping station. You haven't 'forced' the issue (or dreamt it would just resolve itself by sending good vibes to it), but devised a solution that uses the physical properties of water instead.

The same process applies to positive thinking. Clearly getting to know the real subconscious reasons behind our troubles isn't that simple. Sometime, as we have also hinted before, you may need to get more in-depth professional help. However, before you think of getting this kind of help you may like to experiment with a simpler approach first.

Instead of just forcing yourself to think positive about a 'bad' situation, pick a simple and enjoyable aspect of it first, however small this might be (just like a bucket in a big pond!). In job terms say you love a small side of your day to day duties (e.g. book-keeping), but you hate anything else in your work. Don't try changing everything at once, like moving jobs or other drastic measures. Develop that skill you really like much further instead, then offer it freely

...Just work!

and abundantly to family, friends and even the community at large. You can (you will!) think positively while doing all that, embracing the experience with passion and soon you will see a change. This change of perspective can either be very gradual to be almost unnoticeable or a true epiphany, regardless things will start falling into place. So start small, but whatever you do start by getting real pleasure from it, revive and revitalise yourself in the process and above all else, share, share, and share more (or, give, give, give more!).

...One final hint - the new economy

We don't want to sound alarmist or enter into a subject which is by definition alien to the purpose of this book, but think about the world and what's happening to it right now. Just as you can perceive it as a place full of uncertainties with old patterns disintegrating in front of your eyes, you can also see it as a new world of opportunities. Sustainability, green energy, eco-living, you name it, opportunities are there. There are people who have successfully created services where there were none, like 'unmarriage' ceremonies for example. Others have found rewarding careers retraining into alternative healers, or even authors - the choice is almost infinite.

Who said you have to grow conventionally? **Be unconventional if this is what makes you feel fulfilled. Be brave, be yourself, but above all, be passionate, for work and passion are intertwined.** You will not be fulfilled until you have lit the flame of passion for what you create in your heart. We leave you with these few words:

...Work is love made visible. And if you cannot work with love but only with distaste, it is better that you should leave your work and sit at the gates of the temple and take alms of those who work with joy. For if you bake bread with indifference, you bake a bitter bread that feeds half a man's hunger...

Khalil Gibran, The Prophet, 1923

www.ingramcontent.com/pod-product-compliance
Lightning Source LLC
Chambersburg PA
CBHW051806170526
45167CB00005B/1896